SCIENCE TECHNOLOGY ENGINEERING M

STEM Fun!

MY STEM DAY
SCIENCE

Anne Rooney

CARLTON KIDS

THIS IS A CARLTON BOOK
Text, design and illustration ©Carlton Books Limited 2019

Published in 2019 by Carlton Books Limited
An imprint of the Carlton Publishing Group
20 Mortimer Street, London W1T 3JW

All rights reserved. This book is sold subject to the condition that it may not be reproduced, stored in a retrieval system or transmitted in any form or by any means, electronic, mechanical, photocopying, recording or otherwise, without the publisher's prior consent.

A catalogue record for this book is available from the British Library.

ISBN: 978-1-78312-429-9
Printed in China

Design Manager: **Emily Clarke**
Editorial Manager: **Joff Brown**
Executive Editors: **Selina Wood and Nancy Dickmann**
Design: **Jake da'Costa and WildPixel Ltd.**
Picture research: **Steve Behan**
Production: **Nicola Davey**
Editorial Consultant: **Jack Challoner**

AUTHOR
Anne Rooney writes about all kinds of science for children and adults. When not writing books, she can be found getting muddy hunting for fossils, or travelling around Europe by train looking for dinosaur museums and the best chocolate ice cream.

STEM CONSULTANT
Jack Challoner has a degree in physics and trained as a science and maths teacher before moving to the Education Unit at London's Science Museum. He now writes science and technology books and performs science shows in museums and schools.

ILLUSTRATOR
Dan@ KJA-artists Daniel has been a designer and illustrator for more than 16 years, with his work featured in national magazines and newspapers, on websites, album covers, adverts, prime time TV and giant billboards. He's rarely seen without a pen, crayon (he has 3 small children!) or strong coffee in hand.

Every effort has been made to acknowledge correctly and contact the source and/or copyright holder of each picture, and Carlton Books apologizes for any unintentional errors or omissions, which will be corrected in future editions of this book.

Adult supervision is recommended for all activities.

SCIENCE Technology Engineering Maths

STEM Fun!

MY STEM DAY

SCIENCE

Anne Rooney

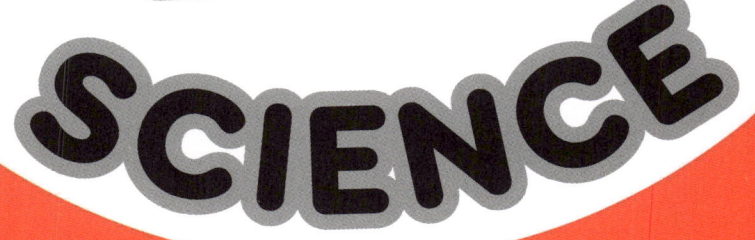

CARLTON KiDS

CONTENTS

LEARN HOW YOUR LUNGS WORK!

What is STEM? 6
Wrap up warm! 8
Ice-cube challenge 10
Brilliant brekky................... 12
Disgusting digestion 14
Let's get going! 16
Super slide 18

Seeing the light................... 20
Tell the time from the sun 22
Kitty snacks 24
Puzzle activity 26
Work that body! 28
Working hard...................... 30

Ice cream chill-out 32
Solid to liquid and back 34
Watering the plants 36
Stringy or strong? 38
Stick'em up! 40
Magic magnet bird 42
In the bath 44
All afloat 46

FIND OUT HOW PLANTS BREATHE!

Bedtime! 48
Make a mini water cycle 50
A goodnight drink 52
Sorting the sand from the sea 54
Getting dark 56
Make your own planet! 58
Science everywhere! 60
Quiz time! 61
Puzzle activity answers 62

5

WHAT IS STEM?

STEM is everywhere in our everyday lives. But it's not all about flowers! STEM is short for **Science**, **Technology**, **Engineering** and **Mathematics**.

Have you ever wondered why ice-cream melts, or turned a tap on for a drink of water or looked up at the stars at night? If so, you've already come across **STEM**. Scientists and engineers over the years have used their understanding of the world around them to develop tools, structures and processes that we use every day.

Are you curious about the world around you? Do you love to ask questions and try out new ideas? Maybe you're a whizz at spotting patterns, solving problems and finding out how things work. If you try something that doesn't work out the first time, do you try again with a different approach? If so, you'll love the world of **STEM**.

Science is one of the four branches of STEM. It is all about investigating the many mysteries of the natural world – even the mystery of you! It can be anything from looking for alien life in the Universe or working on a cure for cancer. Scientists carry out experiments to test their theories.

We depend on science in our daily lives. Without science we wouldn't have lighting in our homes, cars to travel in or an understanding of what clouds are. Once you know where to look, you'll spot examples of science everywhere you go!

What about the rest of STEM? Well, **Technology** is all about making useful devices and finding new ways of doing things. **Engineering** is solving problems to create structures and machines. **Mathematics** is the study of numbers and shapes. These subjects work together to explore and create incredible things!

THE STEM DAY TEAM

SCIENCE   TECHNOLOGY   ENGINEERING   MATHS

Wrap up warm!

When you wake up, you're probably snuggled under your duvet to keep warm. During the day, clothes keep you warm. Have you ever wondered how that works?

The loose fibres inside a thick winter coat help to trap air and keep you warm.

Warm clothes are made of fabrics that are good insulators. Heat can only pass through them slowly, so they slow down the rate at which your body loses heat. Thick fabrics are better insulators than thin fabrics and clothes that trap air in their fibres or between layers are best for keeping you warm.

Heat tends to even out. A hot surface loses heat to cold air and a cold surface warms up near a source of heat. Your body loses heat to cold air, warming the air. If you trap the warmed air near your body with clothes, you'll lose heat more slowly.

warm → cool

feather from a duck

Some duvets are filled with feathers to trap air. Feathers keep birds warm in the same way. Polar bears have hollow hairs so every single hair can trap air! Air isn't the only good insulator. Animals that live in cold places often have a layer of thick, insulating fat.

polar bear hairs, seen through a microscope

Sometimes you need to keep cool, not warm. A fan moves air over your body. Heat from your body warms the air around it, but the warmed air is whisked away and cooler air comes along, so you lose more heat.

You also lose heat by sweating. As water evaporates (turns to a gas) from your skin, it takes heat away from your body. A dog pants for the same reason – it loses heat as water evaporates from its tongue.

Ice-cube challenge

You will need:
- 20 identical ice cubes
- 5 sealable plastic bags
- 4 different materials to try out as insulators, such as: bubble wrap; fabric; newspaper; aluminium foil
- a measuring jug
- a clock or stopwatch

Have you ever brought ice cream home from the shops and found it's half-melted? This challenge might help you to keep it frozen next time!

WATCH OUT! ICE CAN BURN

What to do:

1. Put four ice cubes in each bag, then seal the bags.

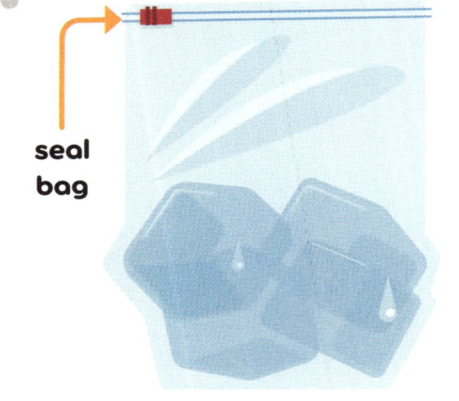

seal bag

2. Wrap one bag in bubble wrap, one in fabric, one in newspaper and one in aluminium foil.

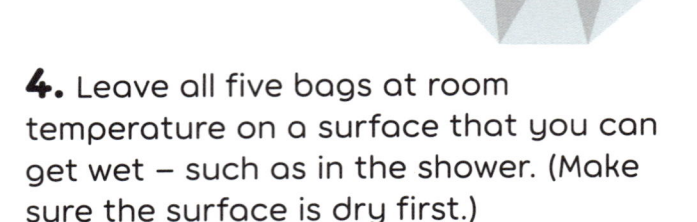

4. Leave all five bags at room temperature on a surface that you can get wet – such as in the shower. (Make sure the surface is dry first.)

3. Leave one bag unwrapped.

5. Check your bags every 10 minutes. As soon as the unwrapped ice melts, unwrap the others. Open the first bag and pour the liquid water (but not the bits of ice) into the measuring jug to see how much there is. Write down the amount. Then do the same for the other four bags.

water

The less water there is, the less ice has melted and the better the material is as an insulator. You may have found the bubble wrap worked well. Why do you think that may be?

Puzzle activity

Draw on some clothes to keep Jess and her dog warm in the snow. Then add some more animals that might live in a cold place. You can make up some animals if you like. What keeps them warm?

Brilliant brekky

Have you ever noticed that sometimes when you wake up your stomach starts to rumble? This is your body's way of telling you that it needs food.

Food provides you with the energy and nutrients that you need to grow, repair your body and keep going through the day. Nutrients are grouped into different types. Most foods contain nutrients from more than one group.

NOM! NOM!

Fruits and vegetables provide vitamins and minerals, which keep you healthy.

Bread, rice and pasta contain carbohydrates, which give you energy.

Fish, meat, eggs and beans contain protein, which helps your body repair and grow.

Oils, butter, nuts and avocados contain fats, which give you energy and insulate you from the cold.

Rice, fruits and vegetables contain fibre, which helps keep food moving through your gut.

1. Your teeth break food into little pieces as you chew and your saliva makes it mushy. When you've swallowed it, a special acid in your stomach breaks it down even more. Powerful muscles in the stomach wall churn your food like a mini washing machine.

2. The food passes from the stomach to the small intestine – a long, curled tube. In adults this tube is 6 m long!

Here, most nutrients are removed from the food and passed into your blood, ready to be carried to the other parts of your body.

saliva

stomach

large intestine

small intestine

3. The waste that's left over moves into your large intestine. You get rid of it the next time you go to the toilet.

Disgusting digestion

You will need:
- a banana
- two biscuits
- 50 ml fruit juice
- 50 ml water
- a sealable plastic bag
- a pair of old tights
- a bowl
- two paper cups
- a metal skewer

It's easy and fun to make your own model of what's going on inside your body every time you eat. Get set to make your own marvellous mushy mash-up!

WATCH OUT! MESSY

What to do:

1. Break up the banana and biscuits and add them to the bag (your stomach) with the water (saliva) and juice (stomach acid). Seal the bag.

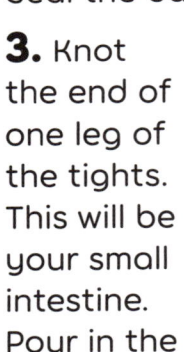

2. Squeeze the bag for a few minutes, like a stomach churning food. The food will start to break down.

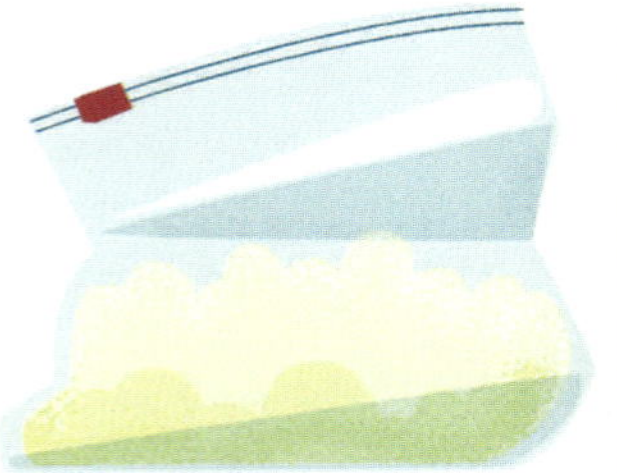

3. Knot the end of one leg of the tights. This will be your small intestine. Pour in the mush.

4. Squeeze the tights over the bowl until most of the liquid comes out. This represents your intestines removing useful nutrients into your bloodstream.

5. Ask an adult to make a small hole in the bottom of one of the paper cups with the skewer. Empty the remaining lump from the tights into the cup.

WATCH OUT! SHARP SKEWER

6. Time to go to the toilet! Place the other cup inside the first one and press the mush out of the hole.

Puzzle activity

Each of these plates has food rich in one important type of nutrient – but there's a food that shouldn't be there on each plate. Can you spot which food is the odd one out?

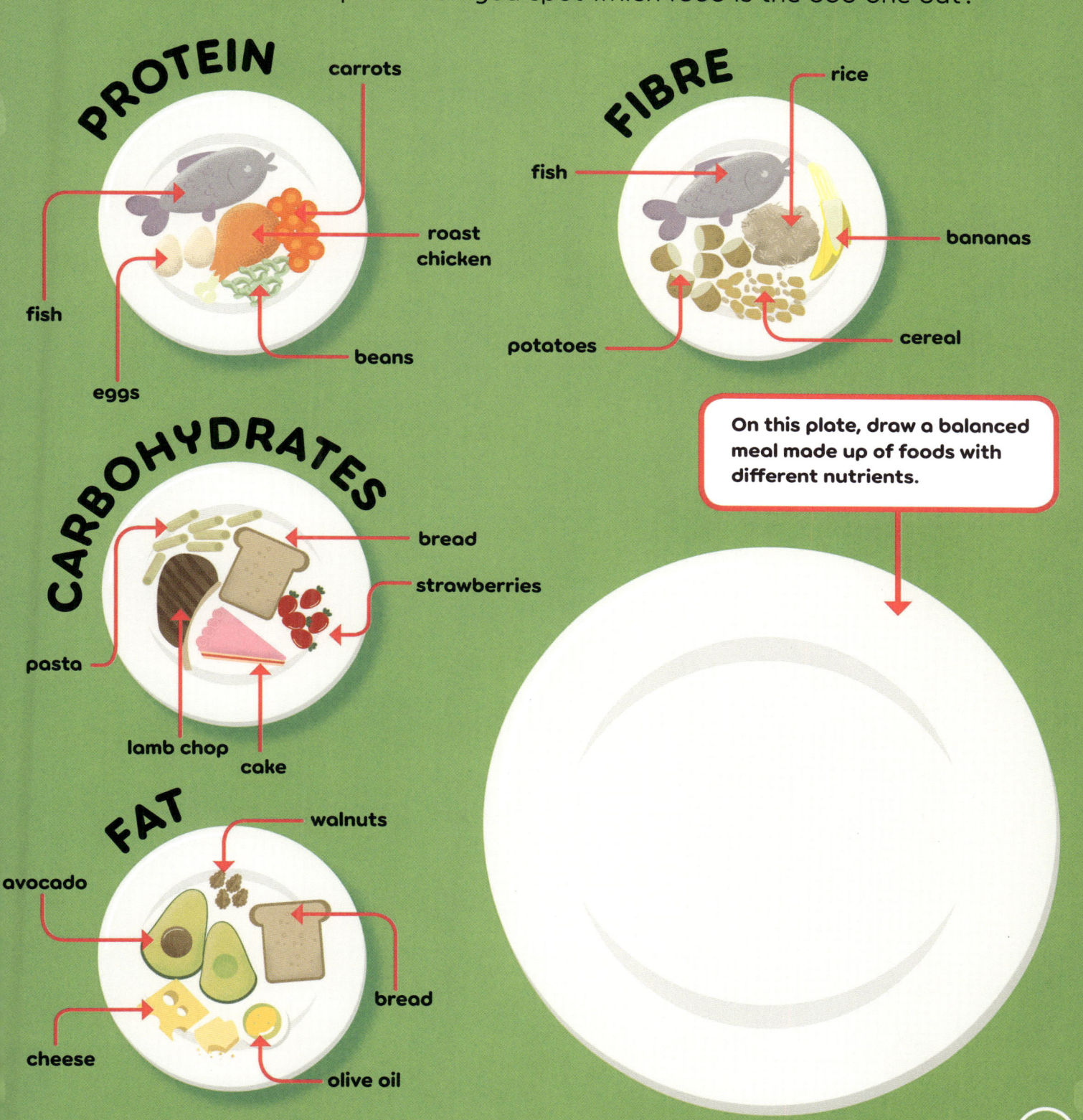

PROTEIN
- carrots
- roast chicken
- beans
- eggs
- fish

FIBRE
- rice
- fish
- bananas
- potatoes
- cereal

CARBOHYDRATES
- bread
- strawberries
- pasta
- lamb chop
- cake

FAT
- walnuts
- avocado
- bread
- cheese
- olive oil

On this plate, draw a balanced meal made up of foods with different nutrients.

You'll find the answers at the back of the book.

15

Let's get going!

Time for school! You might go by bike, scooter or even on your skateboard. To make any of these move, you have to apply a force to it. A force is a push or a pull.

1. Any action produces an equal reaction — this is why a skateboard moves. When you push against the ground with your foot, the ground pushes back with equal force and so you whizz forwards.

2. If there was nothing to stop it, your skateboard would keep going forever. But that doesn't happen — it slows and eventually stops. That's because other forces are at work.

16

3. Wind exerts a force as it blows. It might push you along faster if it blows from behind, but if it's blowing from the front it will slow you down.

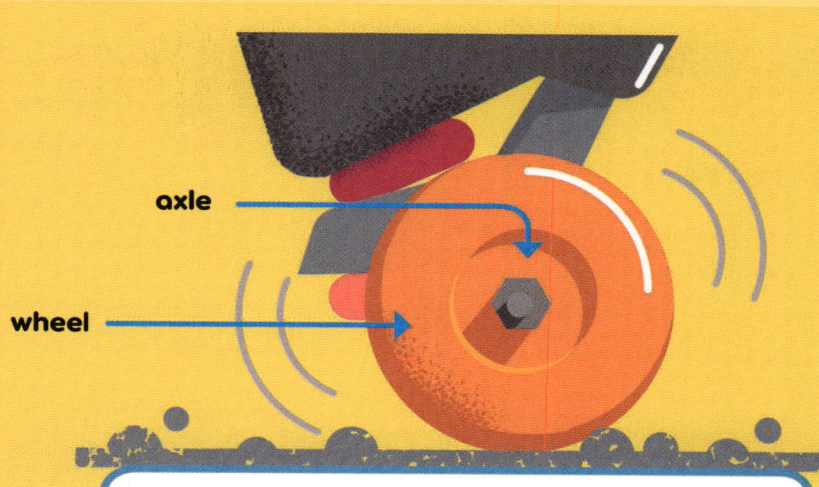

axle

wheel

4. Friction pushes in the direction opposite to a movement. This can slow moving objects. There is friction between the wheels and the ground and the centre of each wheel and the axle on which it turns.

5. Ice is slippery because there's not enough friction with your foot. If you fall over, gravity pulls you to the ground – ouch!

6. Friction turns movement energy into heat. That's why your skateboard wheels get warm. Friction also makes brakes work, and we can use heat from friction to light fires.

rubbing sticks to make fire

7. Air resistance slows you down by pushing against you as you move forwards. Making a streamlined shape reduces air resistance.

streamlined shape

17

Super slide

You will need:
- a friend to help
- a smooth tray
- a few books (to make a slope)
- ice cubes
- a wooden block
- a toy car
- a ping-pong ball
- a ruler
- a hair dryer

You can experiment with forces by making things move – and stop. Let's take a closer look at gravity – the force that makes all things fall towards Earth.

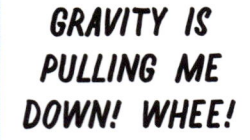

GRAVITY IS PULLING ME DOWN! WHEE!

What to do:

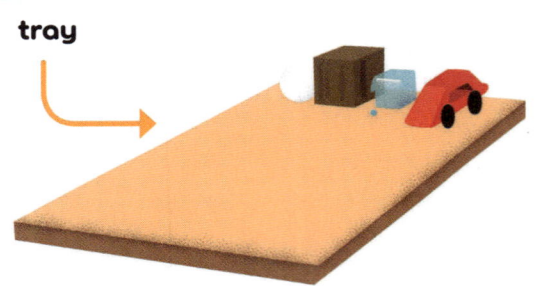

1. Lay the tray flat on the floor and put an ice cube, toy car, ping-pong ball and wooden block at one end. The force of gravity pushes the objects down on the tray and an equal force from the tray pushes back. The two forces balance each other out, so the objects don't move.

2. Give your objects a gentle push with a ruler. This will start them moving, but friction and air resistance stop them. Which object moves furthest?

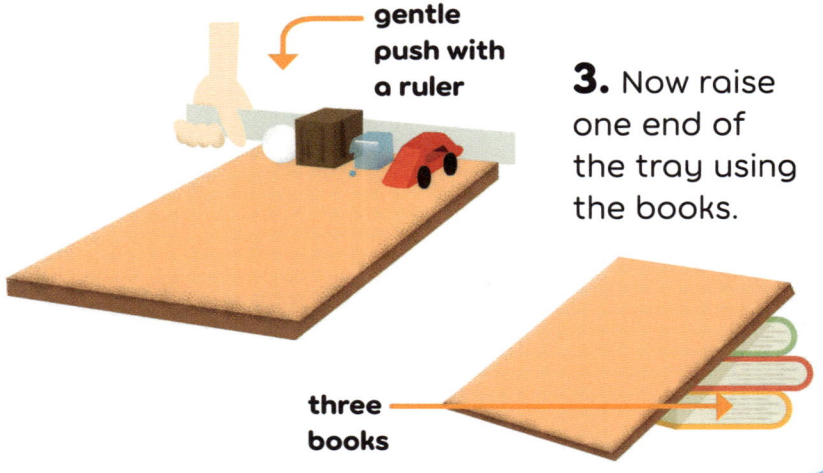

3. Now raise one end of the tray using the books.

4. With help from a friend, line up the ice cube, car, wooden block and ping-pong ball at the top of the slope.

5. Let them all go at the same time. Did they all move? Which gets to the bottom first? Which is the slowest? This time gravity replaces your push, but friction and air resistance slow them down.

hairdryer

6. Turn the hairdryer to cold and blow air up the slope while one of the objects slides down. Can you make the object stop or go back up?

What did you discover? There is most friction between the block and the tray, so that goes most slowly. The ice cube's smooth surface reduces friction. The ball and the car's wheels have a tiny surface in contact with the board, so there's very little friction.

Puzzle activity

Sometimes friction is a nuisance and sometimes it's helpful. Which things depend on friction to work, and which avoid friction?

child on a slide
uses friction ◯
avoids friction ◯

rubbing hands together
uses friction ◯
avoids friction ◯

ice skating
uses friction ◯
avoids friction ◯

sliding on a slippery floor
uses friction ◯
avoids friction ◯

rock climbing gloves
uses friction ◯
avoids friction ◯

sanding wood
uses friction ◯
avoids friction ◯

You'll find the answers at the back of the book.

Seeing the light

Time for a break and the sun's shining outside. Its light lets you see what's around you, as long as there are no objects in the way.

You can't see round corners because light always travels in straight lines. But it can be reflected off objects.
A mirror is a shiny object that reflects all the light straight back.

light goes through glass

light bounces off bear

Light can go through some substances, such as glass. You can see through a glass window — it's transparent. If light can't go through a substance, it's opaque. You're opaque!

Opaque objects cast a shadow because they block the path of light.

20

short shadow

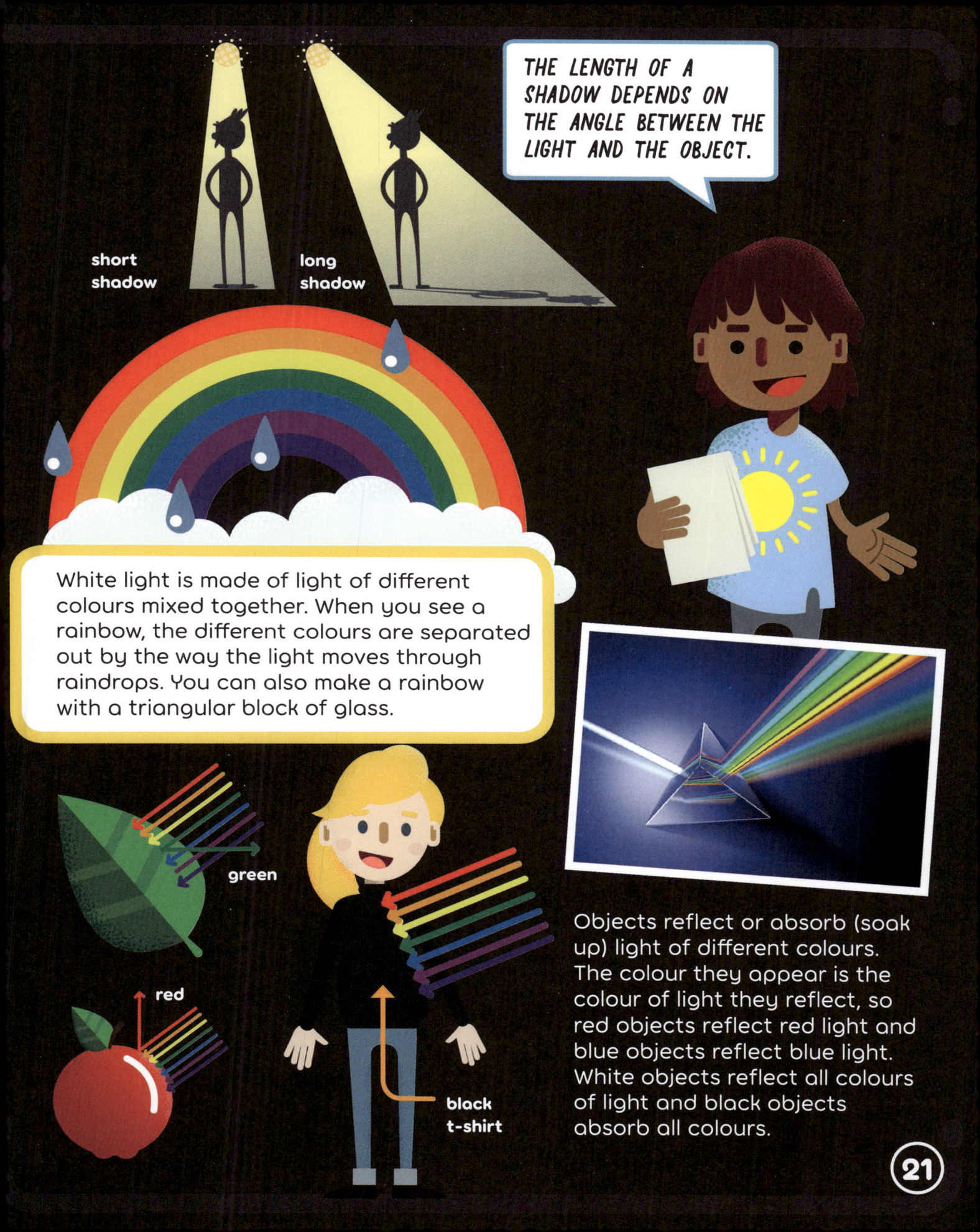

long shadow

THE LENGTH OF A SHADOW DEPENDS ON THE ANGLE BETWEEN THE LIGHT AND THE OBJECT.

White light is made of light of different colours mixed together. When you see a rainbow, the different colours are separated out by the way the light moves through raindrops. You can also make a rainbow with a triangular block of glass.

green

red

black t-shirt

Objects reflect or absorb (soak up) light of different colours. The colour they appear is the colour of light they reflect, so red objects reflect red light and blue objects reflect blue light. White objects reflect all colours of light and black objects absorb all colours.

Tell the time from the sun

You will need:
- a large paper plate
- a marker pen
- a pencil
- a straw or chopstick
- sticky tack
- drawing pins or pushpins
- an adult helper

WATCH OUT! SHARP PINS

Before people had clocks, they often used sundials to tell the time. A sundial uses the length of a shadow cast by the sun to tell you what time of the day it is.

What to do:

1. Push the pencil through the very middle of the plate to make a hole.

push pencil through

2. Using the marker pen, draw a line from the hole to the edge of the plate and write "12" at the edge.

draw a line

3. Take the pencil out and push the straw into the hole, so that most of it is sticking out of the top of the plate.

4. Take the plate outside on a sunny day at noon and put it on flat, soft ground, such as a lawn.

5. Turn the plate until the shadow of the straw falls along the line you have drawn.

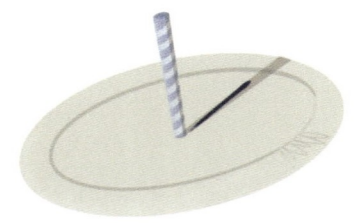

6. If you live in the northern hemisphere, push the straw so that it is slanting slightly towards the north. In the southern hemisphere, push it slightly towards the south.

7. Push the pins through the plate to fix it in place so it doesn't blow away.

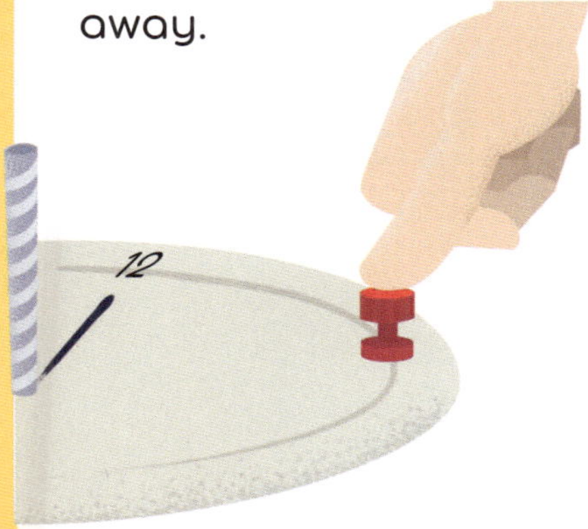

8. The next day, check your sundial every hour and mark the position of the shadow, writing the time on the edge of the plate.

9. You can now tell the time on your sundial from where the shadow falls.

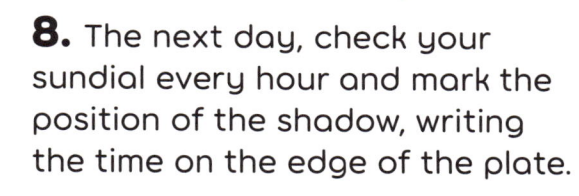

Puzzle activity

Match the violin to its correct shadow. Draw a circle around its letter.

A   B   C

D   E   F

You'll find the answers at the back of the book.

23

Kitty snacks

Lunchtime! No matter what you eat, your food comes from plants or animals. There's a whole web of food and feeding that ties living things together.

All animals need energy from food, including you and any classroom pets. Some animals eat plants and some eat meat (other animals). People can eat either – our bodies can digest both plants and meat.

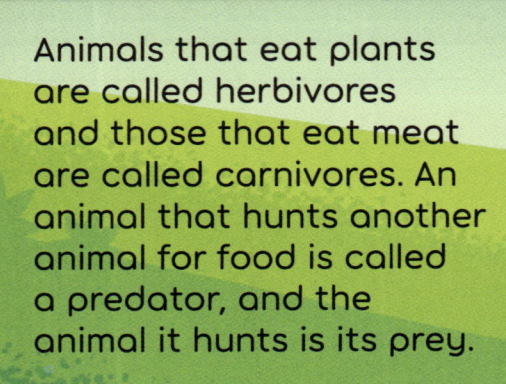

Animals that eat plants are called herbivores and those that eat meat are called carnivores. An animal that hunts another animal for food is called a predator, and the animal it hunts is its prey.

herbivore (prey)

carnivore (predator)

24

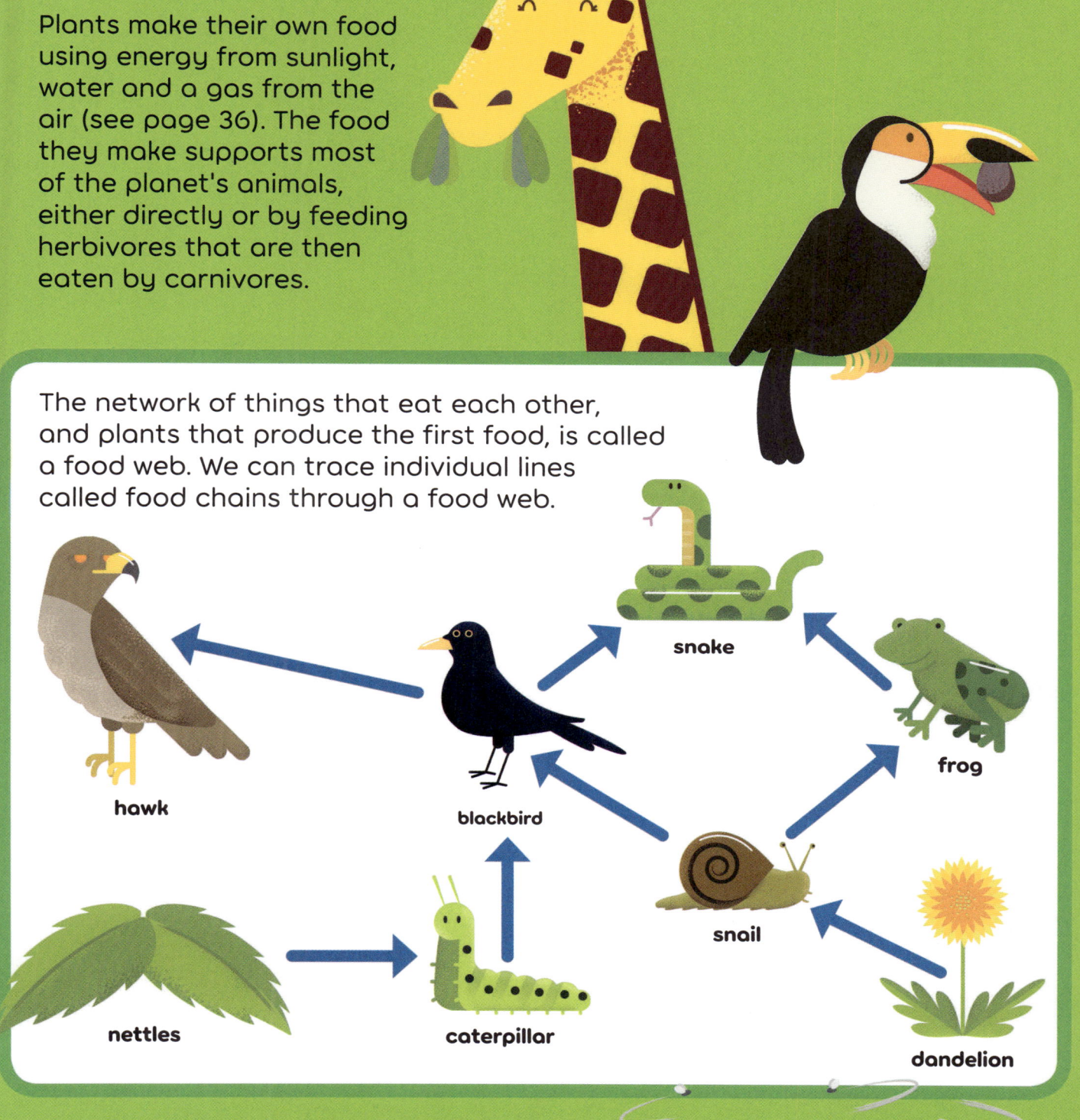

Plants make their own food using energy from sunlight, water and a gas from the air (see page 36). The food they make supports most of the planet's animals, either directly or by feeding herbivores that are then eaten by carnivores.

The network of things that eat each other, and plants that produce the first food, is called a food web. We can trace individual lines called food chains through a food web.

hawk

snake

frog

blackbird

snail

nettles

caterpillar

dandelion

Some animals and microbes (tiny microscopic living things, such as bacteria) eat or break down waste, including things that have died. This recycles them, putting chemicals and energy back into the food web.

25

Puzzle activity

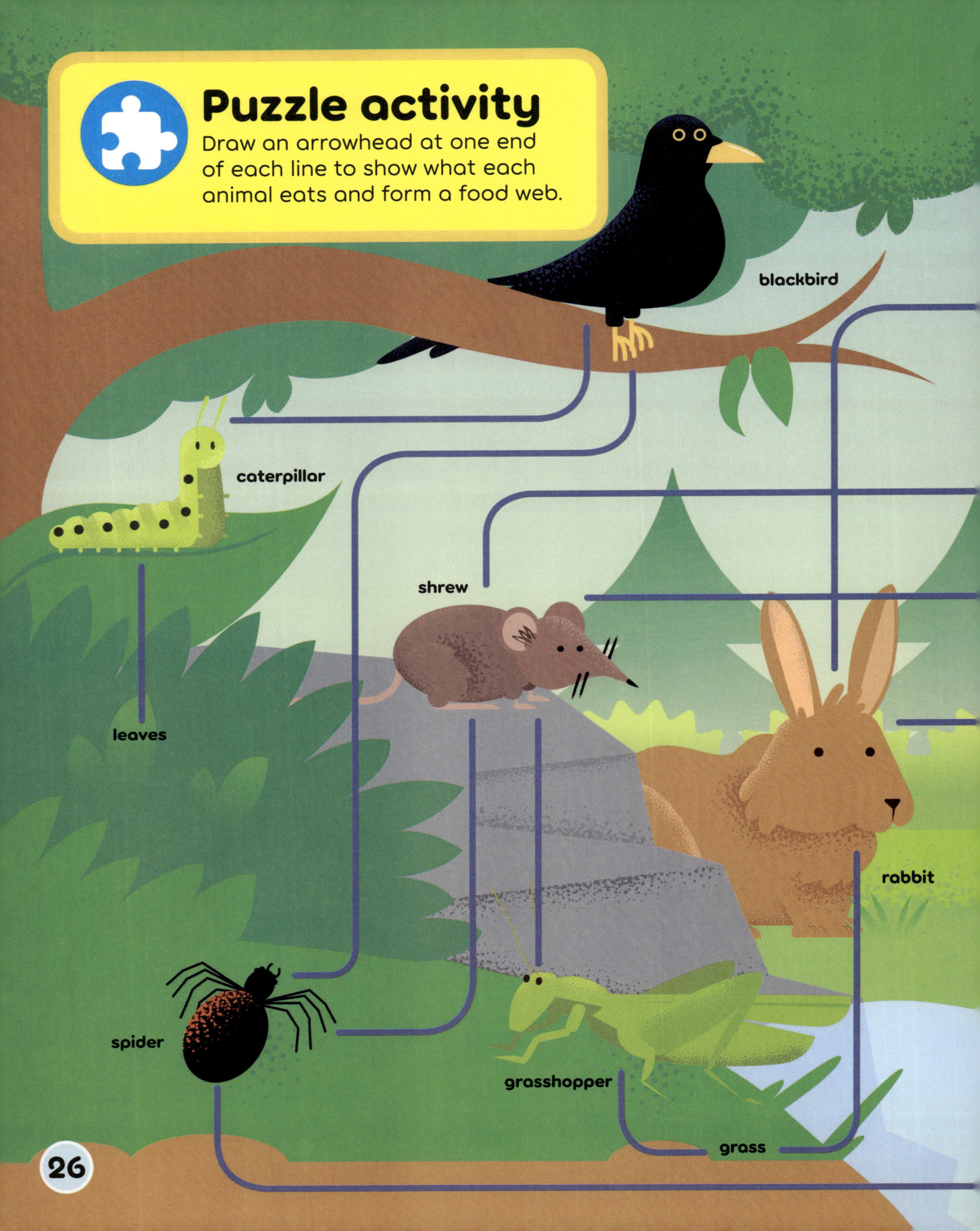

Draw an arrowhead at one end of each line to show what each animal eats and form a food web.

blackbird

caterpillar

shrew

leaves

rabbit

spider

grasshopper

grass

owl

fox

fly

frog

You'll find the answers at the back of the book.

27

Work that body!

Running around in the playground, your muscles move your body, making your heart and lungs work harder than usual. So how does this work?

Your gut breaks down carbohydrates to make a simple form of sugar, which is stored. To break down this sugar and release its energy, your muscles need oxygen, a gas from the air.

When you breathe in, air rushes into your lungs. Your lungs branch into lots of tiny spaces, so their surface area is very large.

Inside your lungs, oxygen passes through the thin walls and dissolves in your blood. Oxygenated blood is blood with oxygen dissolved in it.

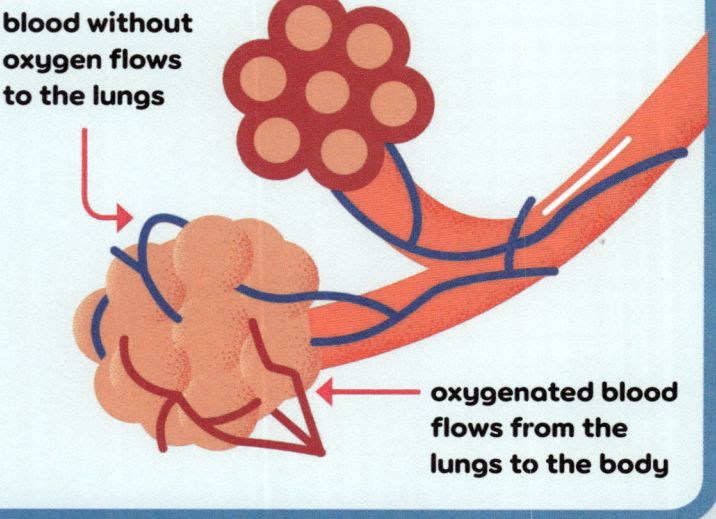

blood without oxygen flows to the lungs

oxygenated blood flows from the lungs to the body

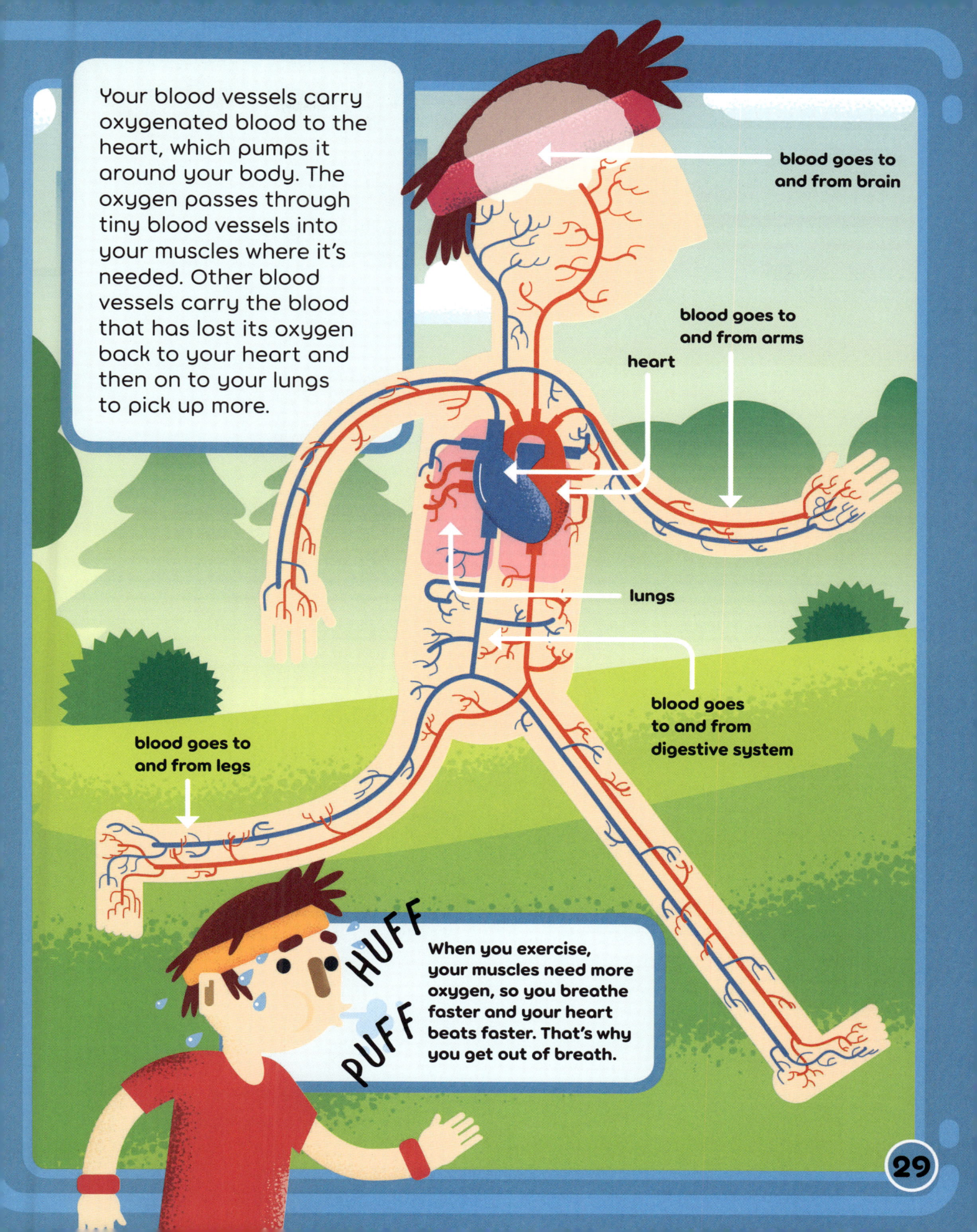

Your blood vessels carry oxygenated blood to the heart, which pumps it around your body. The oxygen passes through tiny blood vessels into your muscles where it's needed. Other blood vessels carry the blood that has lost its oxygen back to your heart and then on to your lungs to pick up more.

blood goes to and from brain

blood goes to and from arms

heart

lungs

blood goes to and from digestive system

blood goes to and from legs

HUFF PUFF

When you exercise, your muscles need more oxygen, so you breathe faster and your heart beats faster. That's why you get out of breath.

29

Working hard

You will need:
- a stopwatch/timer (it can be on your phone)
- a pen and paper

Find out how hard your body has to work when you are active, and then look at just what your lungs have to do.

What to do:

1. Do nothing at all for 10 minutes – that's easy!

2. Put your hand on your neck, a little below the "corner" of your jawbone to find your pulse. Your pulse is the blood being pumped around your body in bursts by your heart beating.

Each "bump" you feel corresponds to a beat of your heart. Count the beats over 30 seconds and double the number to get your heart rate per minute. Write it down.

3. Run around or skip for two minutes. As soon as you stop, count your pulse again. Write it down.

4. Count your pulse every two minutes and make a note of it until it has returned to the rate it was before your activity. How long does it take to slow down?

Did you notice how hard your heart had to work during exercise? The fitter you are the less time it takes for your pulse rate to return to "normal".

And... breathe!

You will need:
- a plastic bottle with the bottom cut off and a hole in the lid
- two bendy straws
- three balloons, one with the neck cut off
- modelling clay or sticky tack
- sticky tape
- an adult to help

You can make your own "lungs" to see how your body draws air in to get oxygen for your blood.

WATCH OUT! SHARP BOTTLE

What to do:

1. Ask an adult to help you partially blow up and release the balloons to loosen them.

2. Put a straw into the neck of each of the whole balloons and fasten them with sticky tape. Fasten the two straws together. These are your lungs.

straws
sticky tape

3. Put the lungs inside the bottle. Push the straws through the hole in the lid of the bottle and put the lid on. Add modelling clay or sticky tack around the straws in the lid to keep them in place.

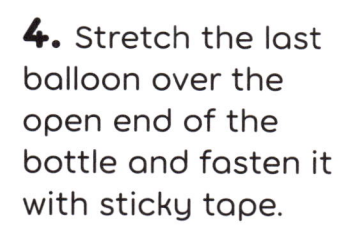

4. Stretch the last balloon over the open end of the bottle and fasten it with sticky tape.

5. Pull with your fingers on the balloon at the bottom and then release it. You will see the lungs inflate as air is pulled in, and then deflate when you release the balloon.

sticky tack

sticky tape

In your body, the work of the bottom balloon is done by your diaphragm, a wide muscle across the inside of your chest.

31

Ice cream chill-out

If it's a hot day you might get an ice cream on the way home. Eat it quickly or it will melt! Why is that? Let's take a look!

Everything can be in one of three states: solid, liquid or gas. Most things are mixtures of two or more of these. A solid keeps its shape. A liquid spreads out and makes a pool if you don't keep it in a container. A gas will spread out in all directions.

solid car **liquid tea** **hot gases**

Everything is made of tiny particles – atoms and molecules. In solids, these particles are held together rigidly, in liquids they are able to move around a bit more and in gases they move around freely!

YUM!

Some substances change their states if you heat or cool them. When a solid changes to a liquid, we say it melts. When a liquid turns to gas, it boils. Iron can melt, but only if heated to a whopping 1,538 °C. You can use a metal saucepan without worrying about it melting!

NOOO!

Ice cream is a mixture of liquid oils in frozen water, with other things, including sugar, dissolved in it. When ice cream melts, the oils remain liquid, the ice melts to make water, and the sugar dissolves in the water. Any bits of fruit are themselves mixtures of solids and liquids.

Change of state is often reversible: many solids can be melted and then frozen again, and a liquid can be heated until it boils and makes a gas, then cooled back to a liquid.

melted lolly

frozen lolly

NOT EVERYTHING WILL MELT OR BOIL. IF YOU HEAT UP LIQUID EGG IT GOES HARD, AND IF YOU HEAT UP A PIECE OF BREAD IT JUST BURNS.

Solid to liquid and back

You will need:
- an adult to help
- an ice cube tray
- a freezer
- olive oil or sunflower oil
- jelly, made with hot water
- butter
- chocolate
- somewhere warm (such as near a radiator)
- paper cups or bowls

Some things that can melt and refreeze aren't quite the same afterwards. If they are mixtures of several substances, the parts might separate out.

What to do:

1. Pour water into one of the ice cube spaces, oil into another of the spaces and jelly liquid into another. Put the tray in the freezer until the blocks are solid.

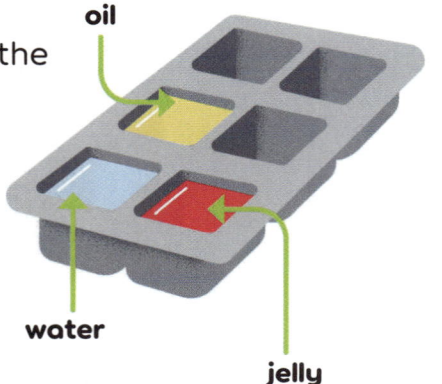

oil
water
jelly

2. Take the tray from the freezer and take out your cubes.

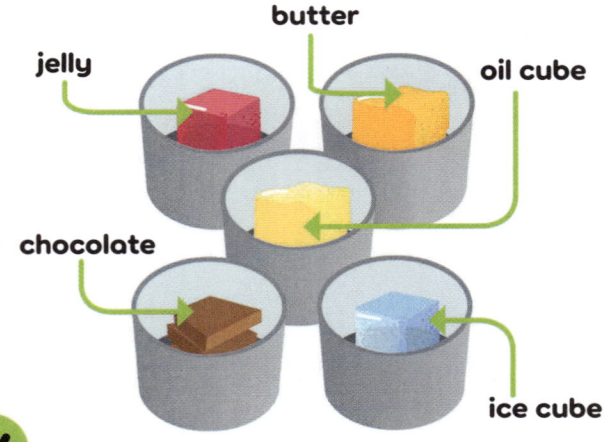

jelly
butter
oil cube
chocolate
ice cube

3. In separate cups or bowls, put an ice cube, an oil cube, a jelly cube, a cube of butter about the same size and two or three squares of chocolate piled up to make a cube of roughly the same size as the others. Put all the cups somewhere warm.

4. Check them every few minutes and notice the order in which they melt.

5. When they have all melted, examine them carefully. What are the liquids like? Are the water, oil and jelly the same as they were at the start?

6. Now put the melted butter and chocolate in the freezer and leave them to go hard. Take them out and examine them. Are they the same as they were before?

SCRIBBLE

The chocolate and butter look different when they refreeze. They are mixtures that separated when they melted. When they refroze, the different parts remained separate. The jelly is a mixture, too, but it doesn't separate when it melts.

Puzzle activity

Which of these things will melt if you make them hot enough? Draw a circle round those that will melt.

| wooden chair | metal spoon | jelly | banana | jumper | cheese |

| ice lolly | fried egg | candle | mug | rubber welly | wax crayon |

You'll find the answers at the back of the book.

Watering the plants

Plants are living things.
If you don't water them they will shrivel and die. On a hot sunny day, they need more water than on a cold and shady day.

Plants don't "eat" like animals do. They take in what they need through their roots and leaves, then make their own food to use.

Plants take in carbon dioxide gas from the air. They absorb water and nutrients from the soil. Using energy from sunlight, they make oxygen and a simple sugar called glucose. They store the glucose and let the oxygen out through their leaves. This process is called photosynthesis.

sunlight
carbon dioxide
oxygen
water and nutrients

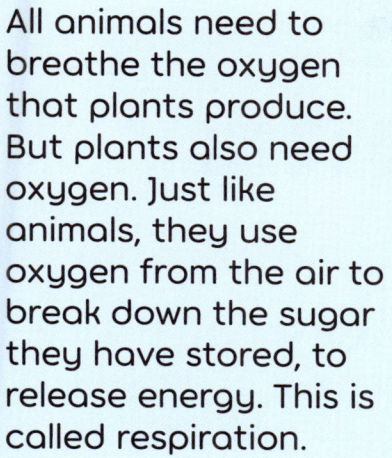

All animals need to breathe the oxygen that plants produce. But plants also need oxygen. Just like animals, they use oxygen from the air to break down the sugar they have stored, to release energy. This is called respiration.

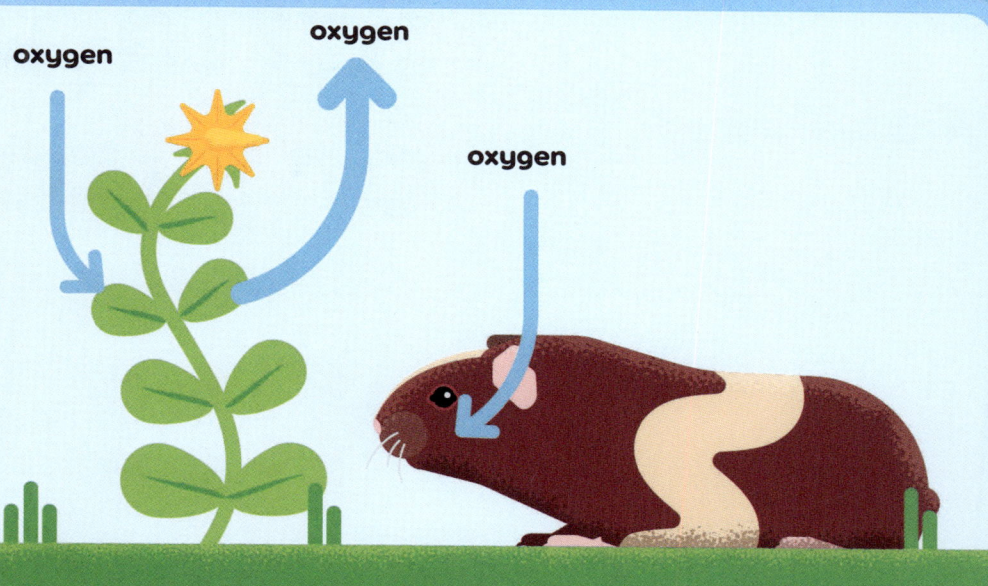

oxygen
oxygen
oxygen

Plants respire all the time, but they only photosynthesize when it is light. Luckily they let out more oxygen than carbon dioxide, so everything keeps going — as long as there are enough plants. But as humans cut down forests and build cities the balance of gases in the air changes.

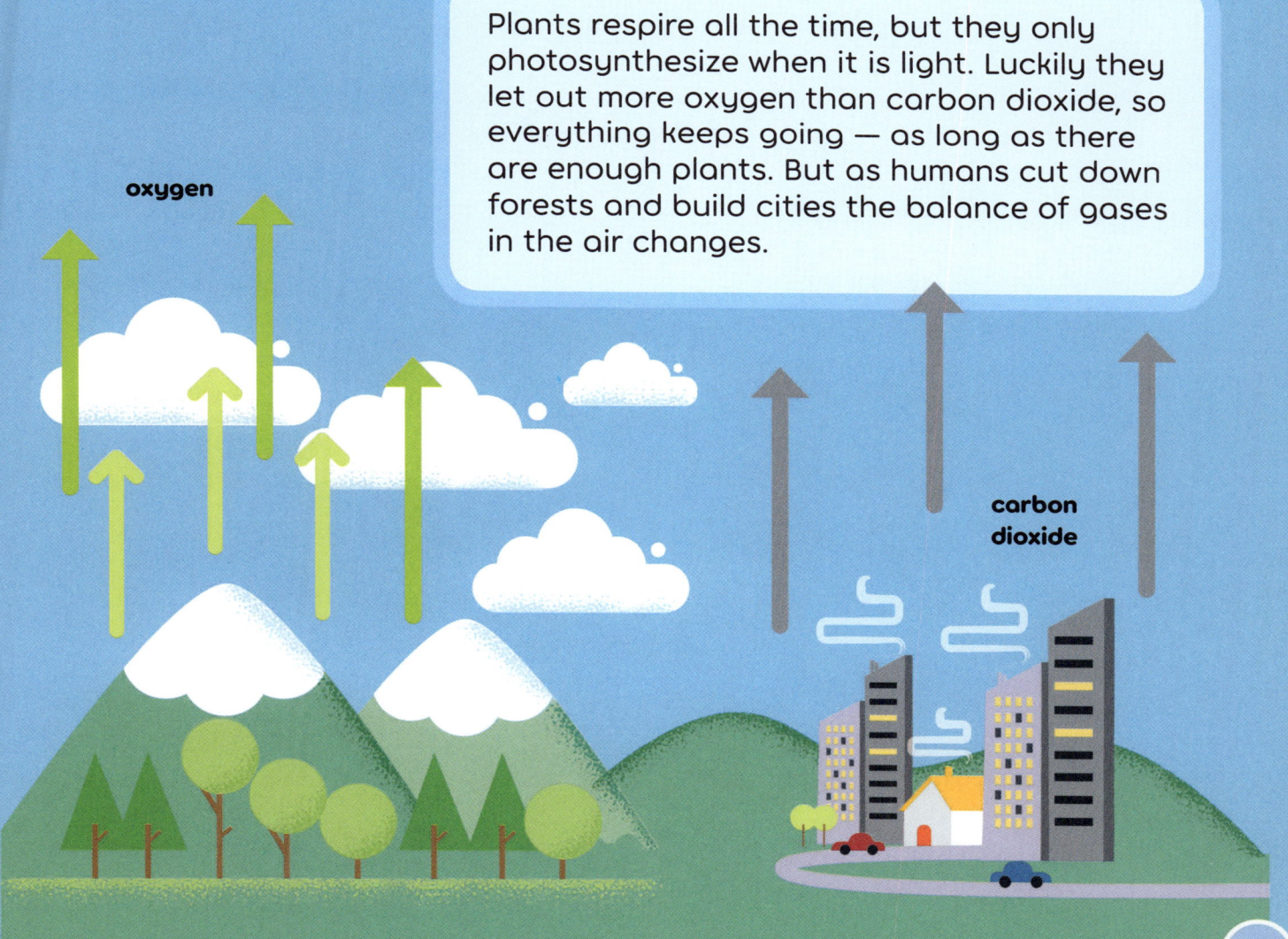

oxygen

carbon dioxide

Stringy or strong?

You will need:
- bean or sunflower seeds
- eight small pots
- soil or compost
- toilet paper or kitchen roll
- water

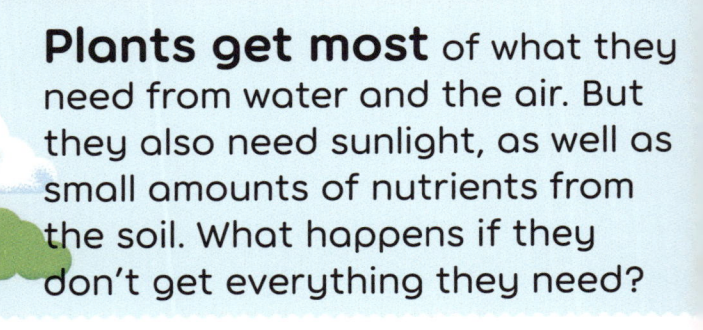

Plants get most of what they need from water and the air. But they also need sunlight, as well as small amounts of nutrients from the soil. What happens if they don't get everything they need?

What to do:

1. Put dry soil or compost into four pots and folded up layers of kitchen roll in the other four. Soak the paper in two pots with water.

2. Push two seeds into each pot of soil and lay two seeds between the layers of paper in the other pots.

3. Water two of the pots with soil. You should now have: two pots with wet soil, two pots with dry soil, two pots with wet paper and two pots with dry paper.

4. Split the pots into two sets, with one of each type in each group: one wet and one dry with each of water and paper.

5. Put one set of pots on a light, sunny windowsill. Put the other set somewhere dark or shady, such as a cupboard.

sunny windowsill

shady cupboard

6. Check your seeds every day for a week. Water the wet plants, to keep the soil and kitchen roll moist. Which plants grow best?

The watered seeds kept in the dark might grow tall and pale. They grow tall because they are trying to find light! The seeds without water in both the light and the dark will fail to grow at all. Seeds can grow in the paper but need soil to get the nutrients they need to keep them alive longer.

Puzzle activity

Find the words that tell you about what plants need and how they grow.

- ENERGY
- LEAVES
- OXYGEN
- ROOTS
- SOIL
- SUGAR
- SUNLIGHT
- WATER

P	S	J	N	S	F	E	E
S	E	R	S	U	G	A	R
E	V	E	Z	N	J	S	O
N	A	T	P	L	O	X	O
E	E	A	T	I	Y	D	T
R	L	W	L	G	K	G	S
G	Y	N	E	H	I	F	X
Y	G	N	M	T	X	N	L

You'll find the answers at the back of the book.

Stick 'em up!

Before supper, you might stick your latest pictures to the fridge with magnets. Have you ever stopped to think why that works? It's pretty freaky, really!

Some forces act between things that are touching. Others act between objects that don't touch. Gravity and magnetism can act over a distance.

Some materials are attracted to magnets and some are not. The magnet doesn't work on paper, but it does work on the metal fridge, so you can trap the picture between the metal and the magnet.

magnet

Many magnets are made of iron, but a few other metals are also magnetic. When they are placed next to objects containing similar metals, these objects become magnetic too. Paper clips can become magnetic, because they contain iron.

magnetised material

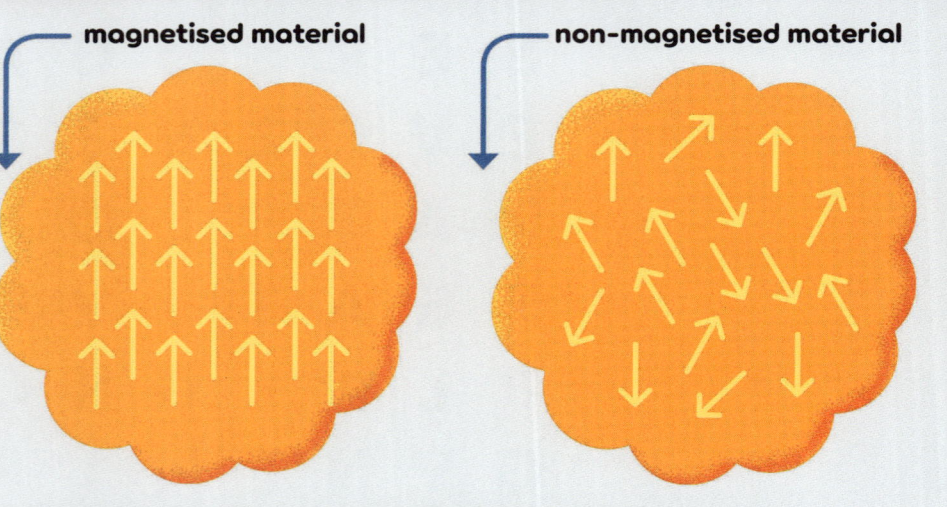

non-magnetised material

A material's different regions each each have their own direction of magnetisation. When a material is magnetised, all of its regions line up in the same direction. Particles in materials like paper or bananas don't line up in the same way.

40

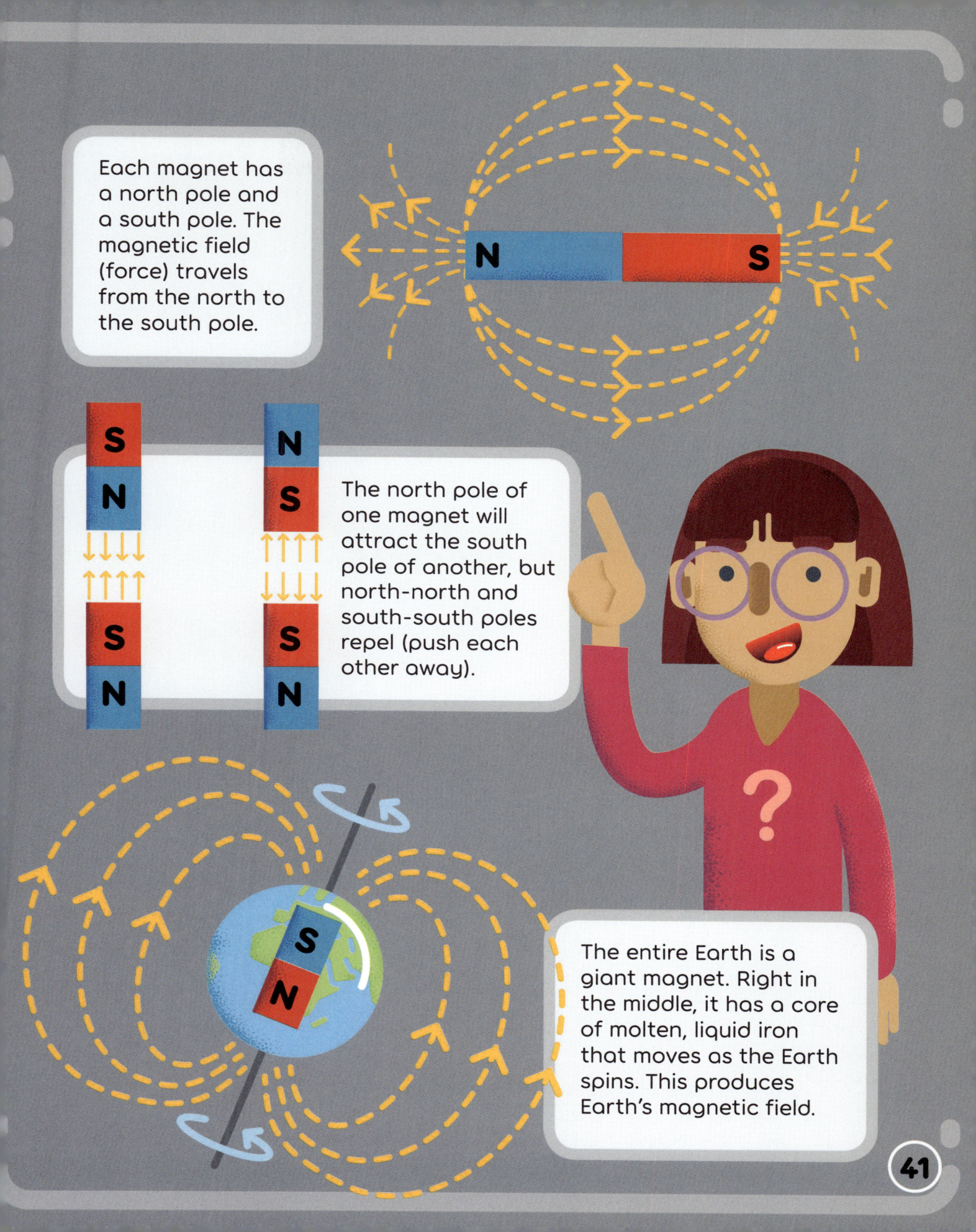

Each magnet has a north pole and a south pole. The magnetic field (force) travels from the north to the south pole.

The north pole of one magnet will attract the south pole of another, but north-north and south-south poles repel (push each other away).

The entire Earth is a giant magnet. Right in the middle, it has a core of molten, liquid iron that moves as the Earth spins. This produces Earth's magnetic field.

41

Magic magnet bird

You will need:
- an adult helper
- a strong magnet
- a small steel paper clip
- paper
- coloured pens or pencils
- a shoebox
- a wooden skewer
- thin thread
- sticky tape

You can do some pretty impressive things with magnets! With a bit of care, you can make things float in mid-air – like this high-flying bird!

What to do:

1. Draw a bird on the paper and colour it in, then cut it out. Attach the paper clip to the bird's wing or head.

2. Tie a length of thread to the paper clip, long enough to go from the top of the box nearly to the bottom.

3. Stand the box on its side with the opening at the front. Decorate the inside of the box with a scene. Ask an adult to help you push a wooden skewer through from one side of the box to the other, near the bottom.

wooden skewer

string

sticky tape

4. Use sticky tape to fix the string to the skewer.

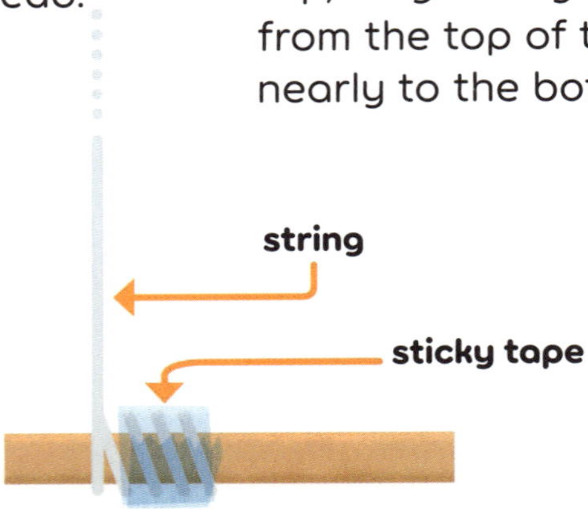

42

5. Hold up your bird, straightening the thread, until it's near the top of the box and put a strong magnet above it outside the box. The paper clip will be attracted to the magnet and stay suspended.

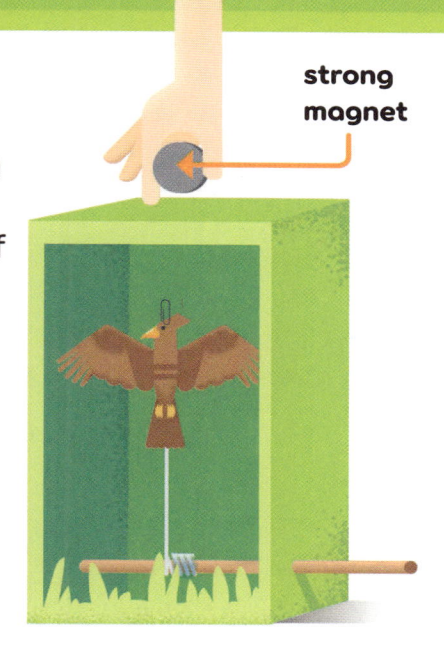

strong magnet

turn handle

6. Turn the skewer to wind the thread around to it. How short can you make it before the magnet can no longer hold up the bird?

WATCH OUT! STRONG MAGNET

Puzzle activity

Which things do you think could be picked up by a magnet? Draw a magnet beside them. You might need a really, really big magnet for some of them!

| tin of fruit | fresh fruit | steel nail | leaf | car |

| t-shirt | aluminium ladder | wooden chair | gold ring |

You'll find the answers at the back of the book.

43

In the bath

A bath before bedtime not only makes you clean and sleepy – it gives you a chance to try out a bit of science!

SPLOSH!

Have you noticed how some things float in the bath and some sink? If you drop a full bottle of shampoo, it probably goes to the bottom, but a nearly empty bottle floats.

Whether things sink or float depends on their density. Density is how much something weighs compared to its volume (the amount of space it takes up).

Things with a high density feel heavy for their size. Those that are denser than water sink; things less dense than water float. And things the same density as water stay suspended in water, going neither up nor down.

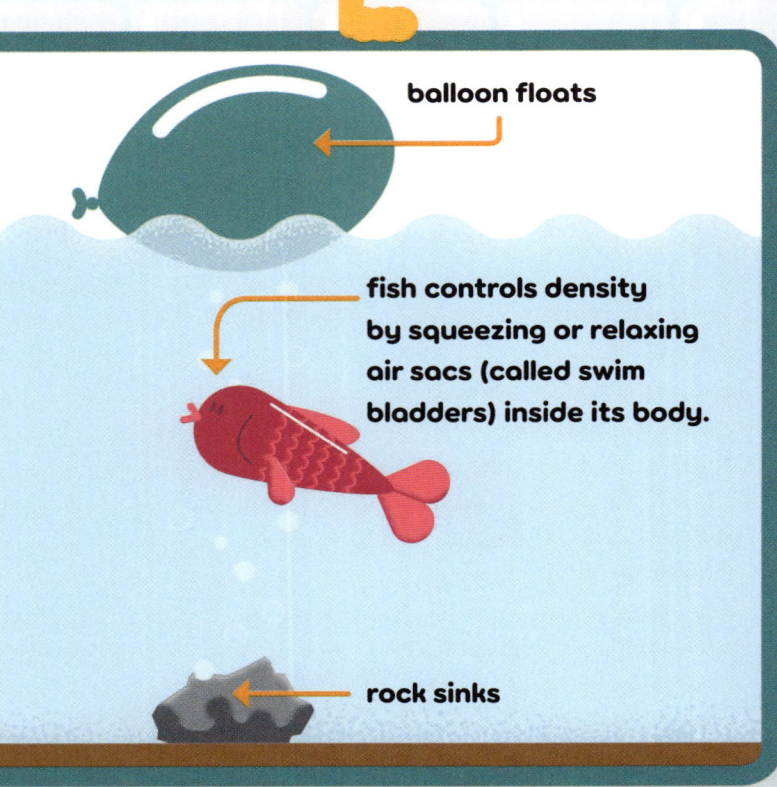

balloon floats

fish controls density by squeezing or relaxing air sacs (called swim bladders) inside its body.

rock sinks

44

The weight of an object pulls it down in the water. But the pressure of water underneath pushes back up, making a force called upthrust or buoyancy.

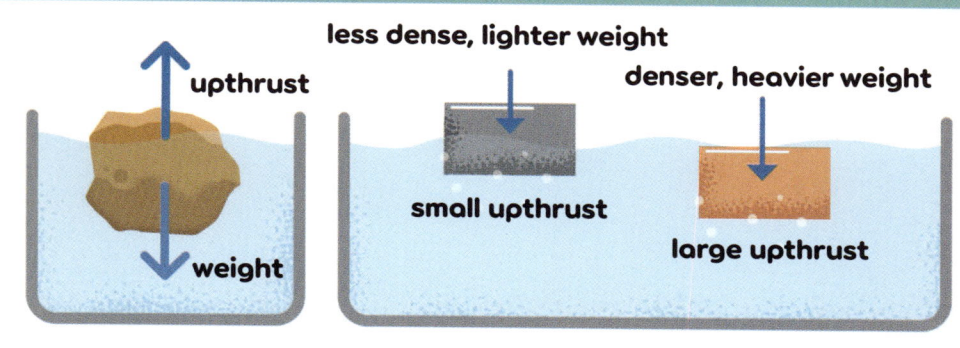

upthrust

weight

less dense, lighter weight

small upthrust

denser, heavier weight

large upthrust

Things float if the upthrust is strong enough to balance the force of gravity. The pressure of the water increases with depth, so the more of the object that is under water, the greater the pressure pushing up on the bottom of the object.

empty metal boat floats high

lump of metal sinks

laden metal boat floats low

Shape can also affect whether something sinks or floats. A lump of solid metal will sink, but a metal boat can float. The boat has a large volume, and a lot of it is taken up with air, so the density is low. The more stuff we put into a boat, the more it weighs. It sinks lower down, until the upward pressure of the water is enough to support the boat.

Some materials get waterlogged or dissolve. You can float a dry sponge on top of bathwater, but once it's filled with water it will go down. A sugar cube sinks in water — and then disappears as it dissolves!

BLUB!

45

All afloat

You will need:
- an ice cube
- a lump of modelling clay
- a sheet of thin wood, or a ruler
- paper
- aluminium foil
- any other materials you can safely get wet
- a large bowl of water, or a sink or bath

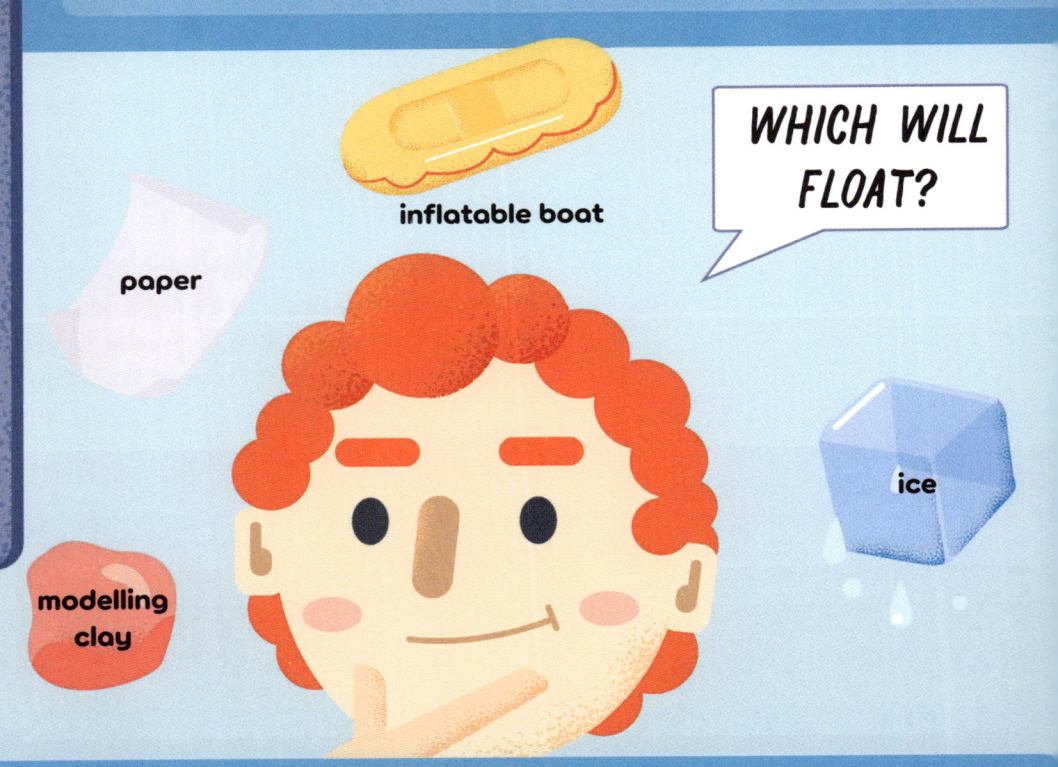

inflatable boat

paper

WHICH WILL FLOAT?

ice

modelling clay

What to do:

1. Scrunch the paper and foil into tight balls.

2. Gently put the ice cube, clay, wood, paper and foil balls onto the surface of the water. Which materials sink and which float?

3. Make a boat shape from each of the materials and put them onto the surface of the water again.

paper boat

scrunched foil

Did you find that some materials floated and some sank quickly? Did any of them dissolve? Did you find some materials sank first but when you made them into a boat shape they floated?

46

Feel the force

You will need:
- a clean plastic bag with no holes in
- a large bowl of water

What to do:

1. Put your hand into a plastic bag and then push the bag under water. The water pushes back against the bag. This is the force that creates upthrust, making things float.

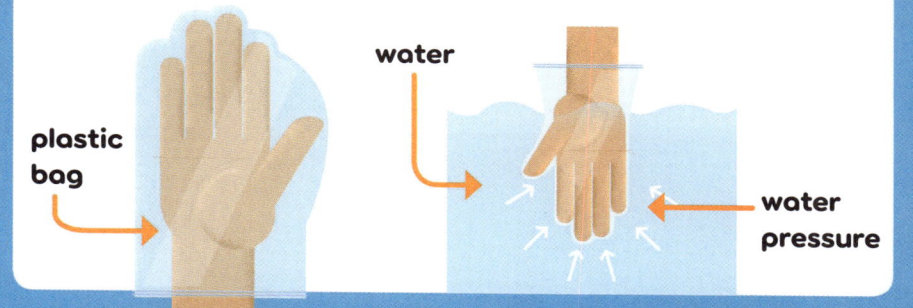

plastic bag

water

water pressure

Puzzle activity

Draw lines from the objects on the left to the level where you think they would be found in the river.

piece of bread

inflatable boat

plate

coin

apple

polystyrene cup

river

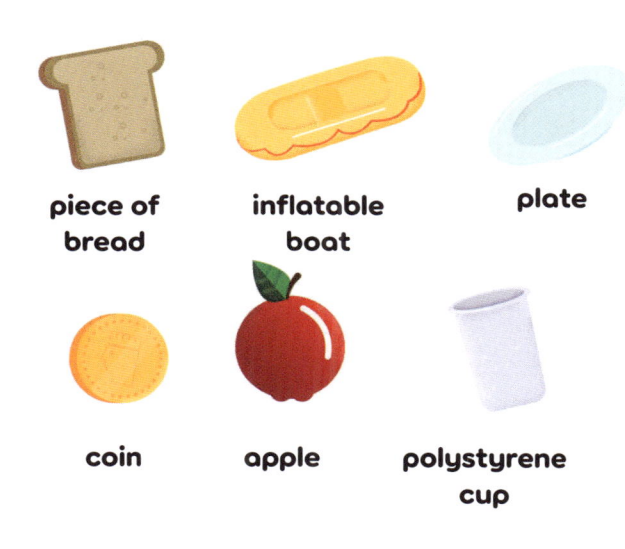

You'll find the answers at the back of the book.

47

Bedtime!

Bedtime is often the wettest time of day! You use water to wash or shower, to clean your teeth and when you flush the loo. Let's take a closer look at the wonder of water...

A tiny drop of water is made of trillions of tiny molecules. Each one has two parts of hydrogen and one part oxygen. Its symbol is H_2O.

oxygen

H_2O

hydrogen

SCRUB!

SLURRP!

Living things depend on water to live.

GASP!

The average person in the UK uses about 150 litres of water a day.

Water covers around **71%** of the Earth's surface, but ocean water is too salty for us to drink.

1. Water falls from the sky as rain onto the land and oceans. Some of the rain that falls on land sinks into the ground, but some collects in gutters, rivers or reservoirs (large lakes built to store water).

2. Rivers carry water back to the sea. From the sea, water evaporates (turns into a gas) and rises to form clouds, starting its journey all over again.

3. Some of the water that seeps into the soil is taken up by plants.

4. Plants lose water through their leaves. The water adds to that in the atmosphere (air), and forms clouds.

5. Plants are eaten by animals — and people — so some water passes through living bodies before returning to rivers or the soil.

6. Water from reservoirs is piped to houses, farms and factories where it's used. Waste water goes through more pipes to be cleaned before it goes back to a river or sea.

town
reservoir
water treatment plant
river
ocean

49

Make a mini water cycle

You will need:
- an adult helper
- a large glass bowl
- cling film
- a cup with a heavy base, less deep than the bowl
- some heavy coins
- hot water
- sticky tape or elastic band

You can make your very own mini water cycle here – with clouds and rain and a sea!

WATCH OUT! HOT WATER

What to do:

1. Put the cup inside the bowl.

2. Ask an adult to help you pour hot water into the bowl, making sure it doesn't go into the cup.

3. Put cling film over the top of the bowl, pulling it tight. If it doesn't stick to the bowl securely, use sticky tape or an elastic band to secure it.

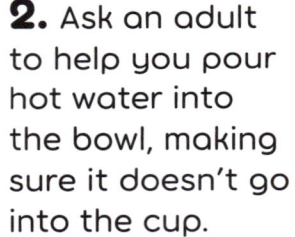

4. Wait. After a while, you should see drops of condensation on the inside of the film. Water has evaporated from your 'sea'.

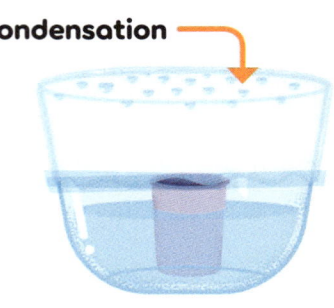

5. Put the coins over the middle of the bowl, on the film. The condensation will collect at the lowest point and fall as 'rain' into the cup.

50

Puzzle activity

Can you find 10 watery words in the grid below? Check out the clues at the bottom of the page to help you...

```
B X H A I L P G A M L K
V P Y D N J L C U O T O
T R A W E L Q P C R P X
A F L O O D B F N E I U
Y Z M G J A H A Q S C R
D E W J W P T S A E P A
N V L S O T H X U R A I
R P R G Q J A Z W V U N
A N I K A B O P A O A S
E W V A S T E A M I I A
E L E D F A Z M G R C A
Q A R X Y C L O U D E A
```

1. Too much water!
2. When water is falling from the sky
3. Carries water to the sea
4. Turn it off while cleaning your teeth to save water
5. Water while it's still high in the sky
6. Water frozen into hard blobs before falling to the ground
7. Water escapes from a boiling kettle as this
8. Large store of water for a town to use
9. Solid water!
10. Water on the grass in the early mornings

You'll find the answers at the back of the book.

A goodnight drink

If you make a cup of hot chocolate or tea, you're dissolving a solid in a liquid, and you're also making a chemical mixture. Who would have thought a drink at bedtime could be so scientific?

Some solids dissolve in water. This means that the solid disappears from view, but it changes the water. It might change the colour, or the taste. It can also change the boiling or freezing point, and the density.

Salt and sugar dissolve easily in water. Things that dissolve in a liquid are called solutes. They usually dissolve more easily if the liquid (the solvent) has been heated. If you try to make hot chocolate using cold milk, you'll find that the chocolate powder doesn't dissolve very well.

undissolved chocolate

The mixture formed by dissolving a solid in a liquid is called a solution. You can often get a solid back from the solution by heating the solution to evaporate the water. You can do this with sugar or salt in water.

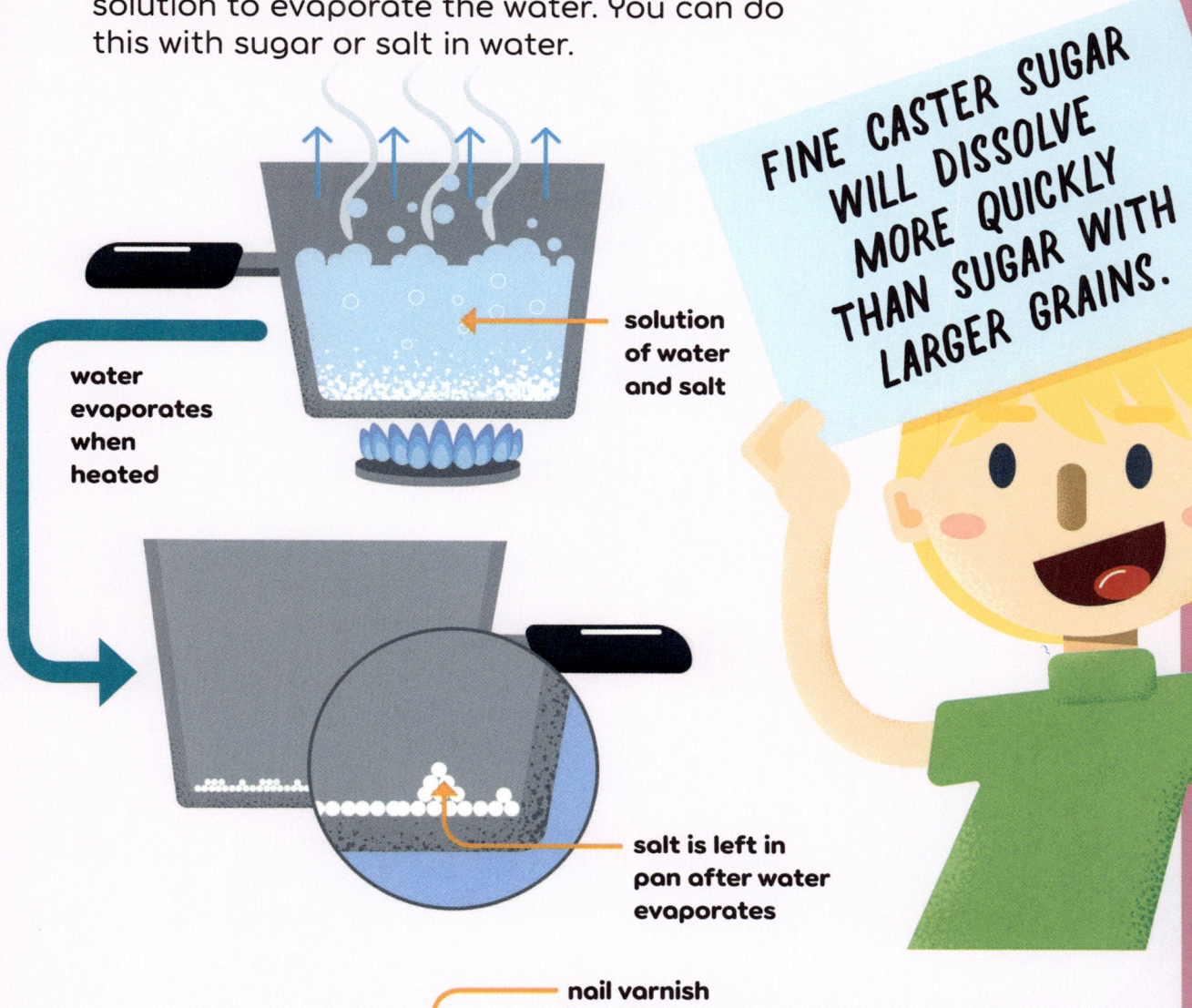

water evaporates when heated

solution of water and salt

FINE CASTER SUGAR WILL DISSOLVE MORE QUICKLY THAN SUGAR WITH LARGER GRAINS.

salt is left in pan after water evaporates

nail varnish remover

Some substances don't dissolve in water, but they dissolve in other liquids. That's why you sometimes use nail varnish remover or paintbrush cleaner to remove stains that you can't get out with water.

Sorting the sand from the sea

You will need:
- sand
- salt
- hot water
- a measuring jug, spoon and bowl
- a sieve
- thin, plain fabric, such as part of an old sheet
- filter papers or coffee filters and a funnel
- a large, shallow dish

The sea is salty water that washes over the sand all the time. Luckily, the sand doesn't dissolve. Can we get the salt out?

What to do:

1. Put two spoons of sand and two spoons of salt into the measuring jug and add hot water.

WATCH OUT! HOT WATER

2. Stir the mixture until the salt has all dissolved.

3. Put the sieve over the bowl and line it with the fabric. Pour the water-and-sand mixture through it. Most of the sand will be caught by the fabric.

fabric
sieve
bowl

54

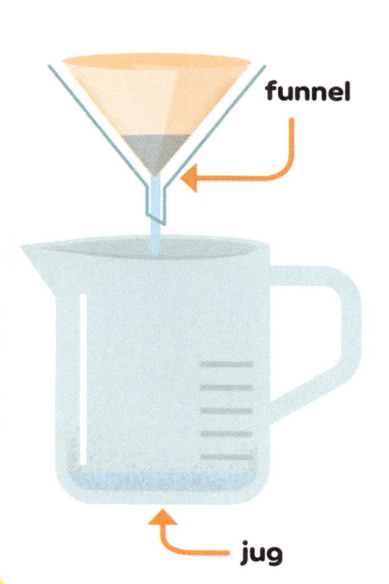

4. Using the filter paper and funnel, pour the water from the bowl back into the jug. The smallest bits of sand, which might have passed through the fabric, will be caught by the paper.

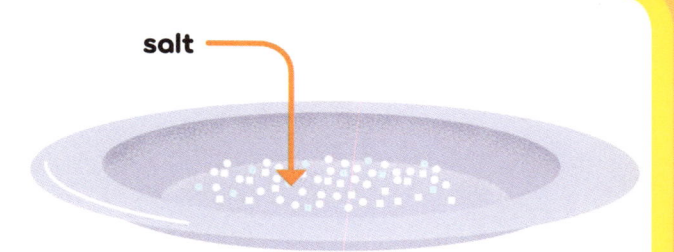

funnel

jug

salt

5. Pour the salt solution into a dish and leave it somewhere warm for a week or so.

What do you notice? As the water evaporates, the salt comes out of solution. It's left as white crystals on the dish.

Puzzle activity

Draw a water droplet around all the things below that will dissolve in water.

LIKE THIS!

paper clip

sugar cube

coloured cake sprinkles

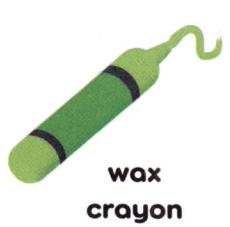

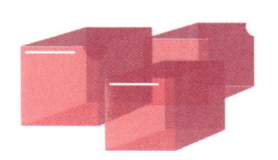

wax crayon

jelly cubes

flour

rubber

instant coffee

You'll find the answers at the back of the book.

55

Getting dark

It's probably dark when you go to bed – unless it's the middle of the summer. When you look at the Moon and stars and Sun, you are looking deep into space!

YAWN!

The Earth is a huge sphere (ball) spinning around in space. As it turns, sometimes the part of the Earth where you live is facing the Sun and sometimes it's facing away. When your part of Earth is facing the Sun, there's sunlight and it's daytime. When you are facing away from the Sun, it's night-time.

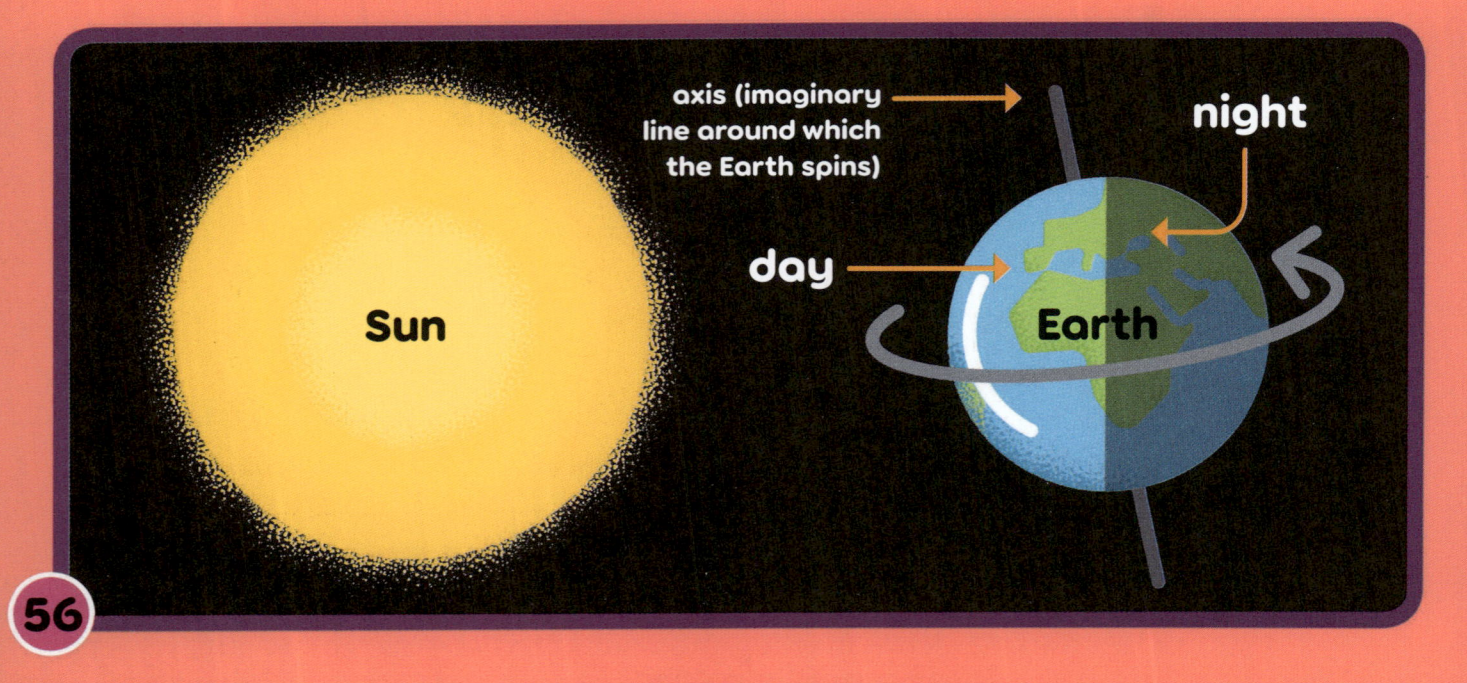

axis (imaginary line around which the Earth spins)

night

day

Sun

Earth

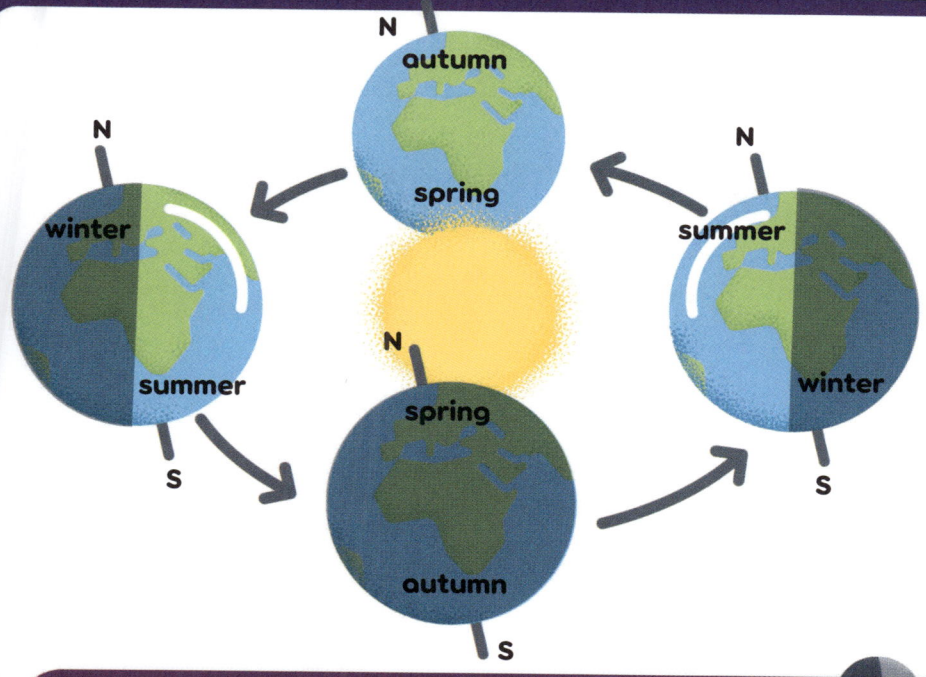

At the same time as turning on its axis, the Earth goes around the Sun. The Earth is slightly tilted on its axis, so part of the year the top half is tilted towards the Sun, and six months later it's tilted away from the Sun. When your bit is tilted towards the Sun, the days are longer and it's summer.

The Moon can appear as a full circle or a thin crescent. That's because when the Moon is between the Earth and the Sun, the side facing us is dark. As the moon moves, we see more of it lit up. The outer circle here shows what we see from Earth.

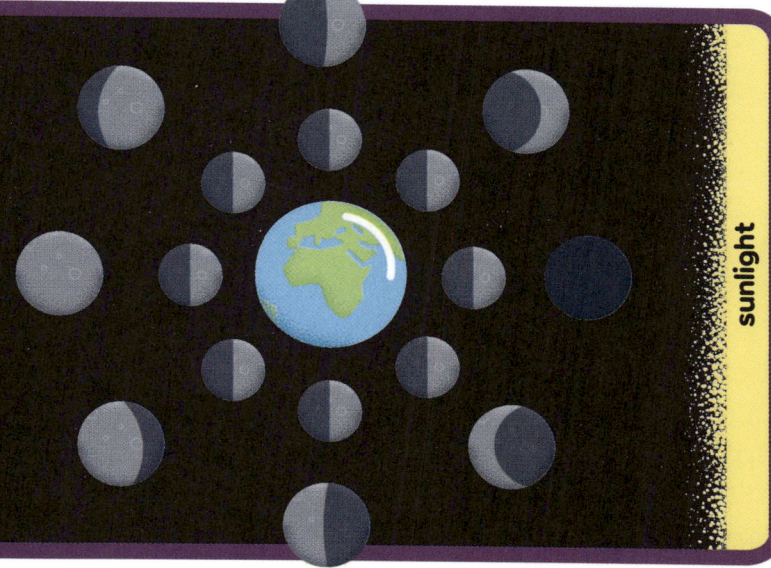

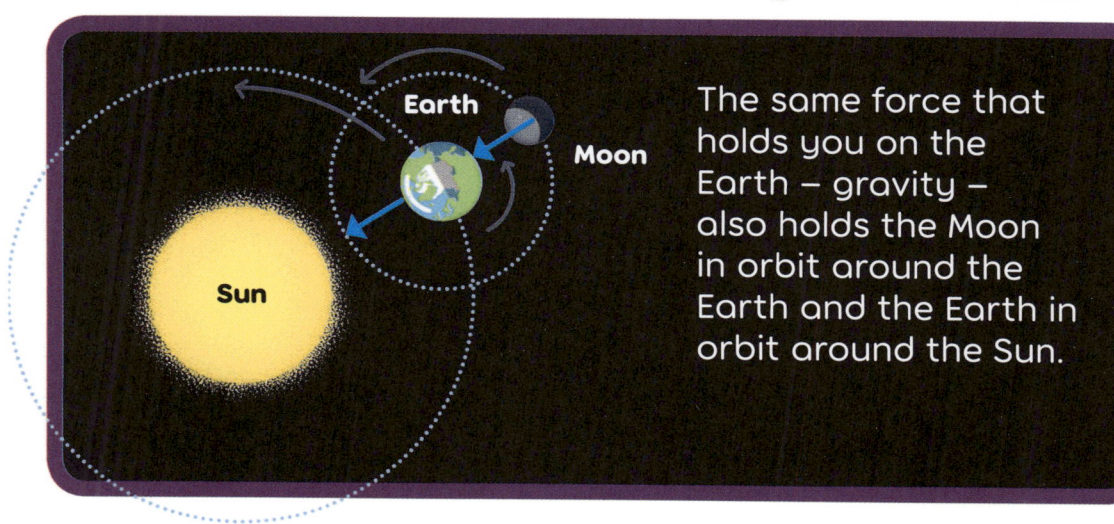

sunlight

The same force that holds you on the Earth — gravity — also holds the Moon in orbit around the Earth and the Earth in orbit around the Sun.

57

Make your own planet!

You will need:
- an adult helper
- an orange
- a skewer
- a marker pen or sticker
- a lamp

Now you can make your very own planet and see for yourself why we have night and day!

What to do:

1. Draw yourself or your country on the peel of the orange, or stick a sticker on it. This represents you on the Earth.

orange

2. With the help of an adult, stick the skewer through your "Earth" from the South Pole to the North Pole.

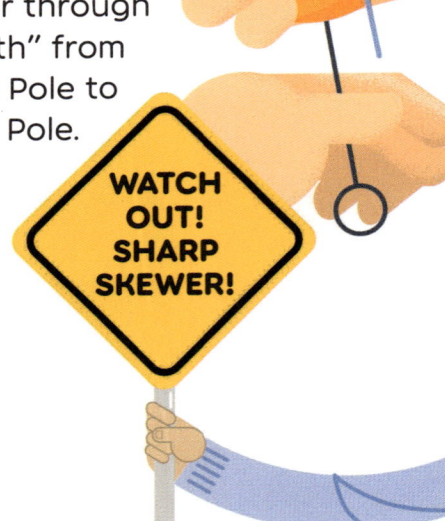

skewer

WATCH OUT! SHARP SKEWER!

3. Turn on the light and hold your Earth-on-a-stick to one side of it.

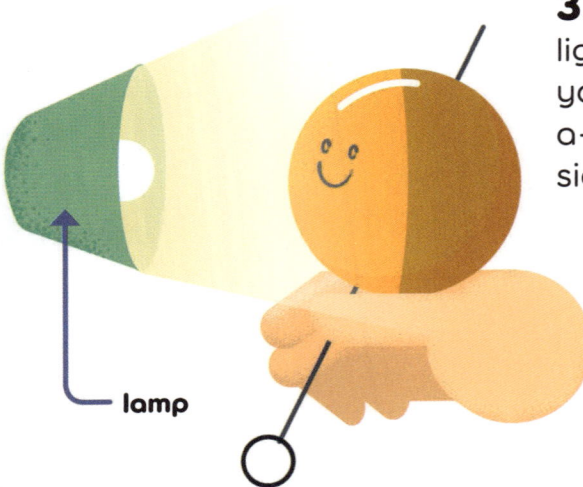

lamp

4. Holding the skewer, turn your Earth on its axis (the skewer) so that it rotates. The side near the "Sun" is in daylight and on the side away from the "Sun" it's night-time.

5. Now draw circles around the top and bottom of the "Earth" near where the skewer goes through.

6. Tilt the top of the skewer towards the lamp and rotate it again. See how the area near the top of the skewer is in the light for more of the time. At the North and South Poles, it is light all day and night for part of the year when each pole in turn is tilted towards the Sun.

Puzzle activity

This alien solar system has four inhabited planets. In which cities is it daytime, in which is it night-time and in which is it dusk? Draw an alien doing a daytime activity or sleeping in night-time in the appropriate circles.

Sun

You'll find the answers at the back of the book.

Science everywhere!

From morning until night, our days are made easier by the work of scientists. Every day, scientists make exciting discoveries that will improve our lives and unlock the world's mysteries.

Imagine life without electricity or medicines to kill germs. Or what if humans had never found out about the force of gravity and how to beat it to reach the moon in 1969? Scientific discoveries have changed the way we live.

Scientists work with engineers and mathematicians to find answers to some of the world's challenges. Will we be able to protect our planet in the future by finding cleaner fuels and plastics that are easier to recycle? Can we find further ways to stay healthy and live for longer?

Think about what you've learned so far about science. Are there any other scientific questions that you'd like to investigate? Where would you start? What questions would your experiments answer? The sky's the limit!

Quiz time!

Test your memory to see if you can remember the answers to these questions about science!

1 Polar bears have hollow hairs because...
a) they can sweat through them ☐
b) the hairs are light ☐
c) the hairs can trap air and keep heat in ☐

2. Which of these food types helps you grow and repair your body?
a) protein ☐
b) fibre ☐
c) fat ☐

3. What is gravity?
a) the force that makes balls bounce ☐
b) the force that makes all things fall towards Earth ☐
c) the force that pushes in an opposite direction to a movement ☐

4. Light always travels...
a) around a corner ☐
b) in straight lines ☐
c) through opaque things ☐

5. Which gas do plants take from the air?
a) hydrogen ☐
b) carbon dioxide ☐
c) glucose ☐

6. Animals that eat plants are called...
a) predators ☐
b) prey ☐
c) herbivores ☐

7. Which of these sets of poles won't repel each other?
a) north–north ☐
b) north–south ☐
c) south–south ☐

8. Things that can dissolve into a liquid are called...
a) solutes ☐
b) solutions ☐
c) substances ☐

Answers: 1c; 2a; 3b; 4b; 5b; 6c; 7b; 8a.

PUZZLE ACTIVITY ANSWERS

Page 15

Protein: **carrots are the odd one out**
Fibre: **fish is the odd one out**
Carbohydrates: **the lamb chop is the odd one out**
Fat: **bread is the odd one out**

Page 19

avoids friction | uses friction | avoids friction | avoids friction | uses friction | uses friction

Page 23

E

Page 26

Page 35

- ice lolly
- candle
- rubber welly
- wax crayon
- metal spoon
- jelly
- cheese

Page 39

ENERGY
LEAVES
OXYGEN
ROOTS
SOIL
SUGAR
SUNLIGHT
WATER

P	S	J	N	S	F	E	E
S	E	V	E	R	S	U	G	A	R
E	N	E	R	E	Z	N	J	S	O
N	A	V	E	T	P	L	O	X	O
E	E	A	T	A	T	I	Y	D	T
R	L	E	W	W	L	G	K	G	S
G	Y	L	N	E	H	H	I	F	X
Y	G	N	M	T	X	N	L

Page 43

- tin of fruit
- steel nail
- car

Page 47

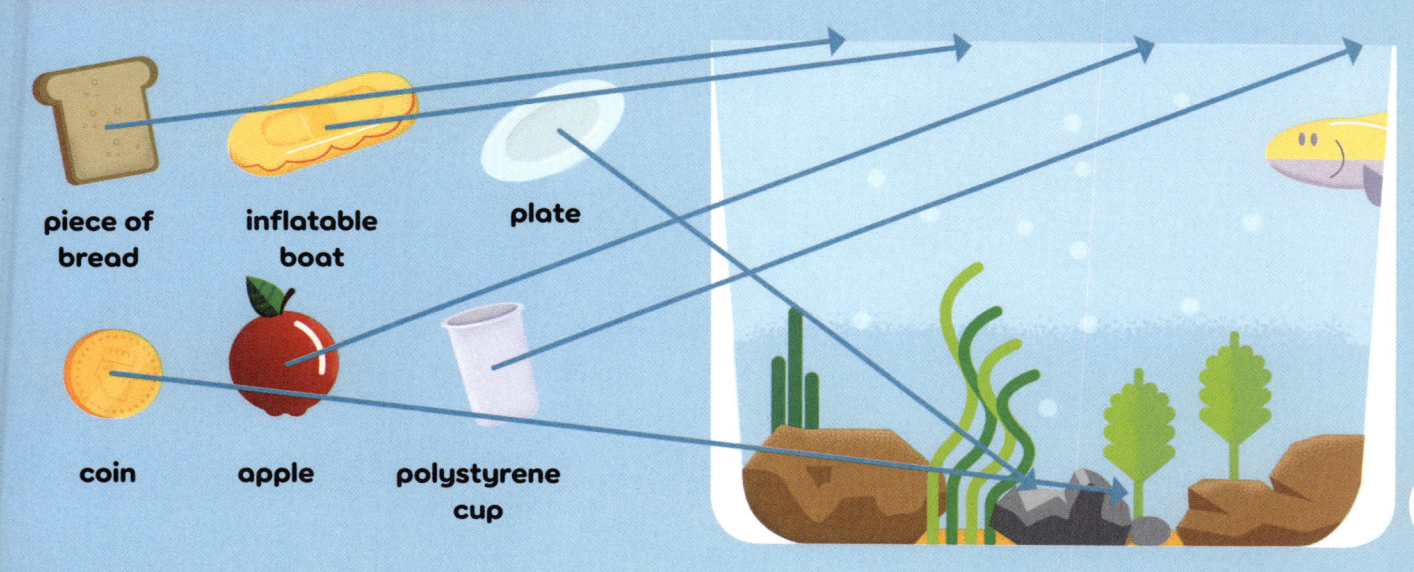

- piece of bread
- inflatable boat
- plate
- coin
- apple
- polystyrene cup

63

Page 51

B	X	H	A	I	L	P	G	A	M	L	K
V	P	Y	D	N	J	L	C	U	O	T	O
T	R	A	W	E	L	Q	P	C	N	R	P	X
A	F	L	O	O	D	B	F	N	Q	E	I	X
Y	Z	M	G	J	A	H	A	Q	S	C	U
D	E	W	J	W	P	T	S	A	E	P	R	A	I	N
N	V	L	S	O	T	H	X	U	R	A	U	A
R	P	R	G	Q	J	A	Z	W	V	U	I	N
A	N	I	K	A	B	O	P	A	O	A	C	S	A
E	W	V	A	S	T	E	A	M	I	I	C	E	A
E	L	E	D	F	A	Z	M	G	R	E	A
Q	A	R	X	Y	C	L	O	U	D	E	A

Page 55

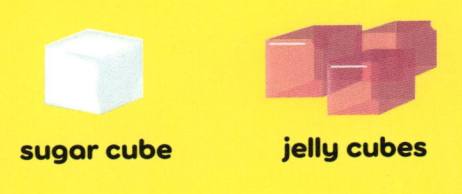

sugar cube   jelly cubes

flour   instant coffee

Page 59

dusk scene

dusk scene

daytime scene

night-time scene